Clear and Simple Guide to
Writing Your College Application and Essay

□
MAX HOLMES

MONARCH PRESS
New York

Published by MONARCH PRESS
A Division of Simon & Schuster, Inc.
Simon & Schuster Building
1230 Avenue of the Americas
New York, New York 10020
MONARCH PRESS and colophon are registered trademarks of
Simon & Schuster, Inc.
Designed by Irving Perkins Associates
Manufactured in the United States of America
10 9 8 7 6 5 4 3 2 1
Library of Congress Catalog Card Number: 84-61102
ISBN: 0-671-52453-4

To my Parents.

CONTENTS

Introduction   7

Chapter 1
The Typical Admissions Process   11
□ Setting the Standards   12   □ Timing: Much More Important Than You Think   16   □ In the Inner Sanctum: Admissions Committee Deliberations   22   □ The Wait List (and the Role of Personal Connections)   24   □ Getting in Through the Back Door: Some Alternate Strategies   31

Chapter 2
Factors in the Admissions Decision   34
□ By the Numbers: An Overview   34   □ The Unique vs. the Well-Rounded   36   □ Grades: Quantity and Quality   37   □ "The Tyranny of Testing"   44   □ Personal Qualities   46   □ Work Experience: Character and the Will to Learn   47   □ Your Application and Essay   48   □ Extracurricular and Community Activities: Crusader or Dilettante   48   □ The Interview: Pressure or Fun   50   □ The Fine Art of Recommendations   52   □ Academic and Career Goals   56   □ Supplements to the Application   56   □ Accidents of Birth   57   □ A Note to Minority Students   58   □ A Note to Older Applicants   59   □ A Note to Foreign Applicants   60   □ A Note to Transfer Applicants   62

Chapter 3
Planning an Effective Strategy: A Step-by-Step Approach 63

Chapter 4
**The Personal Statement: Getting Your Message
Across on Paper 75**
  □ Zen and the Art of Writing an Application 76   □ Topics to Avoid
Like the Plague 78   □ How to Write Effectively and Clearly 80

Chapter 5
Special Admissions Concerns 82
  □ College 82   □ Law School 84   □ Business School 85
  □ Graduate Schools of Arts and Sciences 86   □ Medical and Dental
Schools 87

Chapter 6
Understanding the Admissions Officer: The Human Factor 88
  □ Money: Its Use and Misuse 88   □ The Great Trap: The Pile of Mush
(or, How To Bore an Admissions Officer) 94

INTRODUCTION
How
This Book Can
Help You

The admissions process to colleges and graduate schools is shrouded in secrecy and mystery. Many applicants justifiably view the ordeal as a black box: the applicant sends in a pile of information, a committee of anonymous people using unpublicized procedures reviews the information in total secrecy, the applicant waits in ignorance and with considerable anxiety, and three months later a form letter is generated signalling acceptance or rejection. If one accepts the black box theory, then there is no way to gauge what is on the minds of the decision-makers, and thus all you can do is send in some material and hope for the best.

Other applicants view the admissions process from notions formed by anecdote. Some people who hold this view generalize every admissions process in the United States into a single catch phrase, such as "The way to get into any school is to read their catalog carefully and then sprinkle your essay with references to how interested you are in an area in which they specialize." Sometimes this lore is narrowed down to a particular school, as in, "Yale Law School only takes people who want to become law professors," or, "The way to get into Harvard Business School is to answer the 'Name Your Strengths and Weaknesses' question correctly." Although these beliefs often contain a grain of truth, they are fundamentally misleading. To the weary and confused applicant, they may satisfy a psychological need because they appear to bring certainty, and certainty gives the applicant something to hang on to. But like most universal truths, these catch phrases represent gross oversimplifications, the substance of which crumbles under scrutiny.

The basic premise of this book is that neither the black box view nor the anecdotal approach is correct; any admissions process can be successfully deciphered. As a matter of fact, admissions decisions are highly regularized and often quite predictable. This book will set out what those regularities are. Like all bureaucratic systems, however, the admissions process has its paths of least resistance. The human element is important, and the human discretion factor and the human error factor can be quite large. Since the paths of least resistance—the best routes to travel—also exhibit patterns (admissions officers consistently respond to certain stimuli but not to others), this book will present these tendencies and thus help you make the system work for you and not against you, enabling you to beat the system. This book can help you avoid all of the most common errors applicants make, and can help you steer your essays into the areas that admissions officers respond to favorably most often.

Something should be said at the outset about what this book does *not* plan to do. It is assumed that you already want to go to college or graduate school. There will be no case made for why that would be a good thing for you to do. This book assumes that you are able to decide yourself to which schools you will apply; choosing the right school for you is an extremely personal decision, and no method I could give you could ever be of the slightest practical value.

This book assumes you will be able to master the mechanics of filing the applications; every school has its own set of rules, including things like filing deadlines, maximum lengths for your essays, how many recommendations you must have (and from whom), whether there is an interview, and so on. These requirements vary so widely from school to school that nothing I could say could have any general application. And mastering those formal requirements is merely a prerequisite to getting your application considered. This book is designed to help you with the more sophisticated problem of getting your application accepted.

Finally, this book assumes that once you are accepted at various schools, you will have the common sense to make a good choice, and you will be able to figure out what to do when you get there. The reason I mention these topics which I will not cover is that most other "How to Apply" books on the market are actually filled with fluff on these other topics, and the ten or so pages which do deal with applications give you as much information as you could glean from a careful reading of the explanatory preface of one college's application. This book will give you a great deal of much more detailed information about the admissions process itself, and how you can influence that process to your own benefit.

An early warning: Although any admissions process can be successfully deciphered, that does not mean that any person can get into any school he wants. An applicant must have the qualifications, not necessarily all-star strengths, but at least some. Getting in is always more than just writing a snappy essay and learning a few of the tricks given in this book.

What this book can do is to give you a significant competitive edge. I firmly believe that given two candidates who are roughly equal (in terms of grades and test scores), they can have dramatically different chances for acceptance at the same school depending on the strategies of their applications. This book will coach you toward achieving your full potential in presenting yourself to an admissions committee, thereby enabling you to gain admission to the best possible school.

CHAPTER 1
The Typical Admissions Process

Although every school has its own system, virtually every admissions process is identical in its essential make-up. Universities are generally allowed by law to set their own admissions standards, so long as they do not do something outrageous like denying places to students because they are members of a minority group. (State universities, of course, may be restricted by the state legislature with regard to the number of out-of-state applicants they may accept for any given class.) The power to make admissions decisions is usually delegated by the university to an academic dean, who then delegates it to a committee, on which the dean may or may not sit. Although theoretically the decision of an admissions committee could be overturned at many schools by the academic dean or some higher authority, as a practical matter of university politics this only occurs in the most extraordinary cases.

An admissions committee is usually composed of a full-time director of admissions (often designated Dean of Admissions), several professors, perhaps some assistants to the Dean of Admissions, and perhaps an academic dean or a financial aid officer. The Dean of Admissions, and sometimes some of his assistants, is usually a professional with considerable experience who intends to devote a lifetime to admissions and student counselling. Quite a large circuit exists, around which such lifetime admissions officers circulate from school to school, and sometimes from admissions at colleges to counselling at prep schools.

Many colleges (but very few graduate schools) have large squads of recent graduates who act as assistants to the Dean of Admissions. The chief qualifications for such a job are an undying enthusiasm for the school in order to recruit students effectively (which is most easily, but not necessarily, acquired by actual graduation from the school), and stamina, which is required for the numbing travel across the country in search of candidates, and for the even more numbing task of reading 20–50 applications per day during the decision season. These young assistants often participate, often with a full vote, at admissions committee meetings. Some schools have students serve as advisors to such committees, and a few even allow students to be voting members. But the basic decision-makers are the full-time Dean of Admissions and the various professors who serve on the committee.

Setting the Standards

The first order of business for an admissions committee starting off a new season is to set its expectations for the incoming class. Usually this is accomplished in the summer or very early fall, before the admissions season begins. A meeting is usually held, and a retrospective takes place: a review of statistical trends for the last five years or so on who applied to the school, who was admitted, and who actually matriculated; a review of the previous year's admissions; an analysis of how the school seems to be faring in admissions in comparison with rival schools; and an impressionistic study of whether the last class admitted is a "good, smart group" or leaves something to be desired.

Then the committee sets the standards for the coming season. Most schools, although not all, at this point establish categories based on academic credentials and establish cut-off numbers for each category. Usually three general categories are established, although many more are possible:

Definite Admit: The person will be admitted unless (1) there is a flaw in the application, such as a soft recommendation or an illiterate essay; or (2) the person's personality appears completely uninspiring, and he seems to have no interests outside of studying or getting ahead in a career. At most schools, the Definite Admit group is rarely more than 10–20% of any applicant pool; at Harvard College, for example, roughly 150 out of an entering undergraduate class of 1100 (or 14%) are chosen on this basis; the highest percentage figure I have seen for this group is the University of Michigan Law School, which states in its catalog that 50% of the students it admits are in this category. Academic credentials are usually very narrowly defined. As the University of North Carolina Law School puts it, "Those applicants who rank among the highest and lowest [on the basis of LSAT scores and undergraduate grades] are offered or denied admission primarily on this basis."

Average/Borderline: This person's chances of admission will depend on how he fares in comparison with others in this group; information the applicant provides to the committee is clearly very important in making such distinctions. This is the area of the admissions committee's greatest discretion. There may exist at many schools a subcategory of this category, a "Hold List," where a final decision is delayed until late in the season in order to see how the class is shaping up and how much room is available; the average/borderline category can be 30–60% of all applicants.

Definite Reject: The person's academic record is so weak that (1) there is a presumption that the applicant would have trouble completing the work required by the school; or (2) it appears unfair to allow this person to take a seat instead of someone from the Average/Borderline category. The candidate from this category still has some slight chance of being admitted, but usually only by showing a very unusual personal accomplishment or personality trait, or by demonstrating social or economic disadvantage. Boston College Law School, for example, says very tactfully, "In general, an applicant's chance of admission is quite small if the applicant does not have at least a 3.0 grade point and an LSAT score above the 70th percentile [roughly a 35 on the new exam scale]." This category usually contains 25–40% of all applicants.

Note that these three basic categories are almost always defined by academic credentials alone. (Some colleges factor in a rating for personal characteristics expressed through the application—recommendations, the interview, and extracurricular achievements; some business schools factor in a rating for length and quality of work experience.) For a major law school such as Stanford or the University of Chicago, for example, the numbers might be set as follows: Applicants from respected colleges with both a GPA of 3.5 or above *and* LSAT's of 40 or above are Definite Admits; applicants with both a GPA under 3.0 *and* LSAT's under 30 are Definite Rejects; all others are Average/Borderline.

Please recognize that the schools involved almost never publicly reveal these internal cut-off figures. (Or they will reveal absurdly low cut-off figures to the public, while having a second set of actual cut-off numbers for internal use. They can justify this by claiming that the second figures are only "guidelines" which are not rigidly adhered to in all cases.) In the rare instances in which the guidelines are revealed, the schools go to great pains to minimize them and to emphasize that all sorts of other additional information is used in the admissions process.

You should not be fooled by any of this! Virtually every competitive graduate school, and the majority of competitive colleges, have such a system, and it is very difficult to beat it. If you are in the Definite Admit category, only a blunder will prevent your acceptance. But if you are in the Definite

Reject pile, only extraordinary circumstances can serve to gain you admission. Schools realize that it is generally bad for public relations if they announce strictly defined cut-offs; it shows little concern for the low-grades/scores applicant. In addition, all schools genuinely want the largest possible applicant pool, if only to increase their chances of grabbing that extraordinary applicant, 1 in 1,000, who is a great deal stronger than grades and test scores reflect. But regardless of the propaganda of the schools, a numerical system remains the cornerstone of the admissions process. This is especially true for graduate schools, which now routinely receive five to ten applications for each available space, and which have no choice but to rely on such a system if they want to avoid the monstrous investments of time which a thorough review of each applicant by the entire admission committee would entail.

In addition, students who are in the Average/Borderline category will find that the numerical index will remain the basic determinant of their success in achieving admission. The University of Virginia Law School, for example, has announced that an applicant's GPA and LSAT score will constitute 80% of the decision for that applicant. There is usually a latent belief held by many admissions committee members that there is some unfairness involved in taking someone of lower academic credentials over someone with higher ones. This belief is often not articulated, and sometimes strenuously denied, but I think it lurks beneath the surface of many admissions decisions. When an admissions committee must choose between two applicants in the Average/Borderline category, if neither student has some extraordinary or unusual qualification, and neither has a decided edge in terms of personal characteristics, then the decision will come back to their academic numbers, and the student with the stronger credentials will be accepted.

□**Case History #1:** Tom Franklin* was a senior at Harvard College, and he had long wanted to be a lawyer. He felt that, coming from Harvard, he would have very little trouble finding a good law school to take him, and so he applied to thirteen of the best, including Harvard, Yale, Columbia, Stanford, N.Y.U., and Georgetown. Tom had majored in government at Harvard, which was uniformly recognized as its toughest department in terms of grades (for a number of years Harvard had attached a special letter to the transcripts of government majors, informing graduate schools of the grading standards of the department, but, alas, this program had been discontinued by the time Tom was applying). Tom had a 3.0 average, which was respectable, but, unfortunately, low for law schools used to grade inflation; he also

*In all case histories, the names of the students have been changed to protect the innocent and the guilty. However, the story itself I know first-hand to be true.

had a 650 LSAT score (approximately a 38 on the new scale), overall fair. What Tom did have was outstanding extracurricular activities: He had been an editor of the Harvard *Crimson,* and he had been a leading force in Harvard's Big Brother program in Boston. In addition, he had "walk-on-water"** recommendations from some very highly respected members of the Harvard faculty. The result, Tom failed to make the cut-off at many of the law schools; at the others, his extras were not considered spectacular enough, and in a competition largely based on the numbers he lost; Tom was 0 for 13 and ended up going to Washington as a Congressional aide for a few years before trying again.

The good news is that schools have widely different standards, and one school's Definite Reject can be at the top of another's Average/Borderline category. Only a few schools, such as Harvard Medical School, Stanford Business School, or Yale Law School, have the luxury of setting their standards so high that only candidates with the most outstanding academic records have much of a chance. There are hundreds and hundreds of colleges and graduate schools in the United States, and they maintain an incredible range of academic standards. Except for medical schools, I think it is accurate to say that anyone who can demonstrate that he can do the level of work required can find a place to study.

As an applicant, it strongly behooves you to do some research into the schools to which you are applying, to find out what their academic standards are. You should spend a considerable amount of time thinking about where you would like to go and where you would be satisfied going, and then apply to schools with a fairly broad range of standards. You should anticipate your position on the Definite Admit, Average/Borderline, or Definite Reject scales for each school to which you apply.

Your basic application strategy should differ somewhat depending on where you see yourself on the scales. When applying to a school where you are a Definite Admit, your application should be quite cautious. If you are already a Definite Admit, there is very little need to make the admissions committee even more enthusiastic about you; what you should make sure of is that you say nothing to offend or anger or confuse the admissions committee into reconsidering your status. Your basic strategy should be avoid controversy.

If you are in the Average/Borderline category, your task will be quite different. You will be in with the great majority of the applicant pool, and your job will be to differentiate yourself in one or more ways from it. You

**The phrase is taken from the Bible, and describes a recommendation which says, "This person can do whatever he sets out to do, and in my opinion is one of the best ever."

should focus on exposing the admissions committee to the most favorable aspects of your personality and record, and to presenting your most interesting experiences in the best possible light.

Finally, if you are in the Definite Reject category, your strategy must be much more drastic. You must delve into your life's experiences to present something very extraordinary to the admissions committee, something so extraordinary that it will cause them to lower their usual academic standards to make a special exception for you. Since you have very little to lose, you can and should adopt a high-risk strategy, gambling that the admissions committee will find something very unusual and impressive in your application which will make a compelling case for admission. Again, through use of information given to you by the schools themselves, by counsellors, and by your friends, you must make a realistic appraisal of where you will stand in the applicant pool of each school to which you apply, and tailor your applications accordingly.

Timing: Much More Important Than You Think

After setting the standards for the upcoming class, the admissions committee will set a target number of people they plan to accept. Each school knows what its historical "yield" number is; the yield is the percentage of accepted applicants who actually show up at the school the following fall. If a school's yield has historically been 50%, and the school has 250 seats in its new class, then 500 applicants will be admitted (a yield of 50% is extremely high, except for medical schools; yields of 20–40% are most common.) Such a system based on historical data can lead to havoc if the actual yield for a particular year is significantly greater than or less than the predicted percentage. At the one extreme, colleges have been left scrambling for additional dorm space; at the other extreme, large numbers of applicants are taken from the Wait List at the last minute. (The Wait List is a group of applicants who are neither accepted nor rejected, but rather are required to wait—often to the very end of the admissions process—before a decision is rendered.)

At the end of the first meeting of the year, the admissions committee will make what are basically New Year's Resolutions: each file will get the most careful and thorough examination humanly possible; less emphasis will be placed on standardized test scores this year; the school's standards will remain the same throughout the admissions process, in order to be fair to applicants who apply late in the season. Like most New Year's Resolutions, many of these will be broken within months.

The only resolution which affects particular applicants, as opposed to the pool as a whole, is the third, and it deserves some very careful attention.

There are basically three methods of timing admissions decisions currently in use: rolling admissions, staggered admissions, and single date admissions. Each of these will be analyzed briefly in turn.

One element which the timing methods have in common, in my opinion, is that *as a general rule, the later you apply, the more difficult it is to be accepted.* This is true to some extent at virtually every school, and to a very great extent at some. Now, admissions officers routinely deny in their propaganda that there is a bias toward early applicants. But their job is to defend the process, and that requires claiming that no bias or unfairness infiltrates it. The fact is that such a bias clearly exists to some extent, and it exists as a simple result of human nature.

At the beginning of an admissions process, the admissions committee is faced with a clean slate, on which it can write whatever it pleases. In the early stages of the admissions season, enthusiasm is high. A new class will start to come in, and admissions officers' spirits will rise. Many of the very top students will apply in the very early rounds (since they are often also the most conscientious about punctuality). The admissions committee will begin making final decisions on actual cases, and, if they are on a rolling admissions plan, actually admitting them. Admissions officers will feel generous, since an entire class is open and available. The admissions committee will be slightly more inclined to give candidates the benefit of the doubt. With 90% of the class still open, there does not seem to be a direct connection between admitting one person and denying that seat to another; there is no worry that later some brilliant student will be unable to find a seat, since there are so many available.

Contrast that picture with the situation in March, April, or May. The admissions committee has been working steadily for perhaps six months. Their eyes glaze over each time they look at a new file; something which would have seemed extraordinary in a candidate four months before is now commonplace. A huge backlog of cases has developed, and much less time is available to consider carefully each item in each candidate's file. More and more new applications flow in each day; the admissions officers, already frustrated by the backlog, justifiably are somewhat annoyed with the latecomers, and feel no compunction about according them lowest priority. Decisions have already been made (and perhaps offers already sent out) for 450 of the 500 seats budgeted at the first meeting, and competition for the remaining 50 seats becomes fierce. Candidate is pitted against candidate, and the committee is shy about voting in all but stars to avoid having the precious remaining seats dwindle to nothing. As each acceptance is made, the fear becomes greater that tomorrow's mail will bring a real superstar candidate, and there will be no room for him because the class will be filled.

In addition, by now the admissions committee is presuming that anyone who is completing his application at this late date is disorganized, and might well have some motivational problems. They will not be inclined to give the candidate the benefit of the doubt.

In which category would you rather be?

Perhaps I have overdrawn the picture, but in its essential aspects I think it is accurate for virtually every admissions process. At the very least it is clear that you can never gain an advantage by applying late (except in the very unusual case in which there has been a very significant change in the candidate's record right before the late application), and there may well be increased competition when you apply late.

The most acute case is posed by rolling admissions. Under this method, once the admissions season is formally opened, each file is evaluated as soon as it is complete, and its priority in the lineup is determined by its completion date. The school attempts to make a decision on an applicant some fixed number of weeks after his file is complete, usually within four to eight weeks. A letter announcing the decision is sent virtually immediately, a few days after the final decision is reached. A large number of graduate schools have rolling admissions; Harvard Law School is a good example. It is very clear that under rolling admissions, the sooner you can get your application in, the better off you are. Your application will receive more attention at the beginning of the process, and the admissions committee will have a large number of seats available and thus will be more ready to give a seat to you.

In addition, many colleges and graduate schools have very informal quotas on how many students they will accept from a particular high school or undergraduate college. If you apply late, you run the risk of applying during a year in which the number of students already admitted from your high school or college is over its usual quota, and unless you have outstanding credentials it is unlikely that you will be taken (even though you might have gained admission very easily if you had been the first applicant from your school). The reasoning is, "We usually take only 5 students from Holy Cross each year; this year we've taken 10. We don't want to give Holy Cross the idea that we'll take every candidate they send over here. This candidate is only Average/Borderline anyway, he doesn't have a really strong claim to a spot, let's reject him." Obviously, you should not risk this happening to you; you should be leading your class's charge into college or graduate schools.

The situation is only slightly better at schools which practice staggered admissions. Under staggered admissions, there are a certain number of "rounds" in the admissions process; each candidate who files a complete application by a certain date is considered with the round which starts on that date, and is promised a response at a certain time. Harvard Business

School is a good example: All files completed by November 21 have decisions mailed on January 9; all files completed by January 2 have decisions mailed by February 21, and so on. The last round must have completed applications by April 2 and have decisions mailed on June 4 (please note that these dates change from year to year). In order to maximize your chance for admission, it is absolutely essential that your application be in the first round. A school like the Harvard Business School will in some years fill 50% of its seats from that first round. The chances for the typical candidate in the following rounds consequently become smaller and smaller. Even though the class is kept open into April, the number of students chosen from that round will be a miniscule percentage of the total class.

Why does a school like the Harvard Business School even bother to keep its class open so long? The answer is very simple: Every year they get a few extraordinary candidates who apply very late; usually these are people with incredible work experience, who have very demanding jobs and thus cannot know six or eight months in advance that they will be in a position to leave their posts to enter business school the following September. In order to attract these people and have room for them, Harvard and other graduate schools keep slots open during the spring. But instead of getting 10 applications for every available space, as might happen in the first round, perhaps 40–50 applicants will compete for each remaining seat. Clearly, this is not a position you want to find yourself in.

Finally, there is the single date admissions process where all, or virtually all, acceptances are sent out on a specific date. Virtually all colleges subscribe to such a system, with a date in mid-April chosen as a uniform standard for all applications. Many graduate schools do as well. (Harvard College, for example, gears itself to the mid-April date. The three examples I have used highlight the fact that different schools within a single university system can have completely different admissions procedures.) Is such a system free from the squeeze placed on the candidate considered at the end of the season? Absolutely not. The squeeze is somewhat less severe, of course. But the admissions committee votes on candidates throughout the year, as their applications become complete, and then those acceptances are merely held in the file awaiting the mailing date, which may be many months off. Although theoretically the admissions committee could reverse some acceptances if they see that an end-of-year squeeze is forcing them to toughen their standards, as a practical matter admissions committees are very reluctant to reconsider an applicant on whom they have already voted and on whom a final decision has already been made. Usually, this will be done only if there has been some major change in that individual's file. Consequently, even where there is a single admission date late in the season, it is probably somewhat easier to be accepted if you complete an application early.

Schools attempt to mitigate this effect by creating special hold lists where some marginal and risky candidates are placed in order to defer decision on them until the end of the season. The success of such an effort in large part depends on how skillfully the individual institution is able to use this category. In addition, the late regular applicant is in only a slightly better position; slightly fewer people have been accepted before him, and the hold group will be considered after him if he is not very late. But still, he is being considered long after the bulk of the class has been chosen, at a point where very few places remain open.

Given that you should apply early regardless of the admissions timing system involved, what is the optimal time to apply? Although this may be an unanswerable question, I am willing to stick my neck out on the topic. Your application should be *complete* (including essays, all recommendations, transcripts, test scores, and everything else) by October 1st, or three weeks after the school begins taking applications, whichever is *later*. Why am I this specific? On the one hand, you want to be as early as is reasonably possible. On the other hand, I think you should avoid being one of the very first cases considered. The first couple of dozen applications of any admissions season are bound to get special scrutiny. Everyone on the admissions committee is curious to see how the first files are shaping up. In a great number of cases, there are new members of the committee to be introduced to the entire process, and what better introduction than to go over actual applications with a fine tooth comb. I submit that you do not want to be part of this group. Every person has weaknesses; these weaknesses can only get magnified in such a process. At such an early stage, the committee will probably be just a little bit gun-shy about starting to admit candidates from the Average/Borderline group before there is any indication of how the class is shaping up.

And finally, the very first candidates considered by any admissions committee will be filled with two types of candidates: "holdovers" and the "super-neurotic." Holdovers are candidates from the previous admissions season (often late candidates) who did not make it and are back to try again. Many schools allow holdovers to reactivate their applications automatically simply by filing a new fee; usually, no new essay or recommendation is required. Holdovers are usually weak candidates who are nevertheless very intent on going to a particular school. The admissions committee probably had a reason for the rejection the first time, and it is unlikely to ignore that reason and reverse itself the second time. By human nature, people generally ratify rather than reverse decisions they have made. Unless the holdover has some significant new item to add to the file, he is unlikely ever to be admitted.

The super-neurotic do everything long ahead of time, and every aspect of their applications is in order and as perfect as they can make it. Their only problem is that the word "super-neurotic" is written all over their applications. Their chances will rest almost exclusively on their academic credentials. In no event do you want to risk being found guilty-by-association with either of these two groups. Therefore, to avoid special scrutiny and to be classified at the beginning of the normal applicants, you should wait three weeks, or until October 1st, whichever is later. October 1st is as good a psychological signal as any to indicate the serious start of the real admissions season; it probably takes the average admissions committee three weeks from the start of the season to get ready for serious business.

In order to make these dates, you must be organized. Every school in the country adheres to the Complete Application Rule. What this rule means is that your case will not come before the admissions committee until it is absolutely complete. As a practical matter, your file will probably not even be read by anyone other than clerical staff until it is deemed complete. In order to have a complete application at all schools to which you are applying, you must plan ahead. All of your transcripts should have been ordered and sent during the summer. (Remember that this type of material can accumulate in your files at the schools to which you are applying.) Any standardized tests needed should have been taken during the previous school year, if possible, so that you could retake them during the summer if you were disappointed by your first scores. Taking a standardized test in the fall in which you are applying can easily delay consideration of your file until Christmas, something you should very definitely avoid. You should work on your applications during the summer, write them then, and pull them together for their final versions during September.

Finally, recommendations, which are often the great bottleneck of the admissions process, if at all possible should be solicited during the summer. (An added bonus of applying early is that your recommenders can devote time and attention exclusively to your candidacy. The situation will be very different in the frenzied days in the middle of the admissions season, when they may each have 20 or 30 recommendation forms gracing their desks.) You must plan far enough ahead so that you have a completed file at each school to which you are applying by October 1st, not just the essay portions of the application.

Isn't it true that if you apply early, you may receive a rejection notice early as well? Yes it is true, but that, too, is to your advantage as it gives you more time to make alternative plans. Some applicants appear to have a mystical belief that the longer their application file sits in an admissions office—even if it is incomplete—the better their chances. This belief has no relationship with reality: Virtually all admissions decisions for a particular Average/Borderline candidate are made at a single meeting of the full admissions committee. The only question is whether your file will be included in a meeting early in the admissions season or late in the season. And as we have seen, there are substantial advantages to having your file considered early.

In the Inner Sanctum: Admissions Committee Deliberations

Once the admissions committee has held its initial meeting to set the goals for the class, the admissions season unfolds. The Dean of Admissions and his assistants always conduct an initial screening of the applications and place them in the various categories which have been created, according to the academic credentials the applications establish. At some schools, the dean may have the authority to admit immediately students in the Definite Admit category and reject those in the Definite Reject category. At other schools, a professor or two must read the file before such action is taken. As a practical matter, however, the professors reading such files are basically a rubber stamp for the dean's decision in 99% of all cases.

Applicants in the Average/Borderline category are under additional scrutiny. Usually the file is circulated among several members of the admissions committee, who summarize their feelings about the candidate in a few sentences. Once three to five people have actually read the file, it is ready for review by the full admissions committee. During the admissions season, the committee holds regular meetings, anywhere from once a week to once a month, to discuss pending cases.

At some schools, the Dean of Admissions personally introduces each file, and then general discussion ensues. But at many other schools, a member of the committee is appointed as the advocate for the candidate's file, and has the responsibility of presenting the file in its best light. Other members of the committee appoint themselves as devil's advocates to argue against your admission. Clearly, a large luck factor is introduced at this stage.

First imagine your advocate as a senior professor, perhaps the very articulate chairman of the political science department, whom everyone is slightly afraid of and whom no one wants to argue with seriously. Now imagine your advocate as the student member of the committee, who perhaps has been making a fool of himself in front of the committee all year. Or imagine your advocate as a 23 year old, recently hired junior admissions officer, whose sole goal in life is to please the Dean of Admissions. I am not saying that anyone would be intentionally biased against you because of the identity of your advocate, and perhaps most committees are self-conscious enough to compensate for differing advocacy skills on the committee. But the odds are that luck will play a role here.

There are other luck factors as well: Your file comes up at the beginning of a meeting, when everyone is fresh and sympathetic; your file comes up at the end of a frustrating day, when everyone wants to go home; your file comes up right after someone who wrote a terrible application, so you look good; your file comes up right after a real star, and you look weak in comparison; your file comes up after a string of rejections, and the committee wants to accept someone; your file comes up after a string of acceptances, and the committee thinks it will fill the class too quickly if it doesn't start rejecting people.

The applicant's file is debated; it is passed around the room and people examine parts of it. There may be a comparison of the applicant vis-a-vis others from the same school; there may be a comparison of the applicant vis-a-vis someone with a similar record who was recently accepted or rejected by the committee. Eventually, after five to thirty minutes, some sort of decision is reached. At some schools, a majority rules; at a few it must be unanimous; at a few the final decision is left to the Dean of Admissions, with the vote being advisory. At most schools, a consensus must be reached to admit an applicant. At most schools, voting is done openly through a show of hands to encourage members of the admissions committee to air fully their reservations about candidates they see. Other schools have different procedures. The most bizzare is that of Yale College, where each member of the committee reportedly has a mechanical lever, suitably cloaked by a black cloth cover, through which he can cast his Yea or Nay; the final tally is then electronically transmitted to the seat of the Dean of Admissions.

When the vote is taken, the committee may accept or reject the applicant on the spot (notification of such a decision might come many months later, depending on the school's timetable), or it may defer decision. The deferral could be temporary; you could be put on a hold list, to be examined in a month or two when the committee has a better idea of how the applicant pool is shaping up. Or you could be deferred until the very end of the season by being put on the Wait List. If you are on the Wait List, your fate will be determined by how many people accept invitations to matriculate at the school. Applicants on hold are not usually informed about their status; sometimes the only signal that a candidate is in such a position is an inexplicable delay on the part of the committee. On the other hand, applicants on a Wait List are usually so informed.

With regard to the deliberations of admissions committees, there is at least one major myth which needs to be exploded. Many people believe that admissions systems operate on a quota system, whereby a certain percentage of seats are held open for white men, a certain percentage for white women, a certain percentage for minority men, a certain percentage for minority women, a certain percentage for foreign students, a certain percentage for graduates of certain schools, and so on. Although this is an appealing theory— it seems to explain neatly the rejection of many disgruntled applicants—it has very little basis in fact. To start with, any numerical quota involving race has been declared unconstitutional by the United States Supreme Court in the *Bakke* case. If rigid quotas were ever in effect at any schools, they were based on race, and they are now illegal and no longer used.

If virtually no school has such quotas, formal or informal, why do their entering classes consistently reflect very similar percentages from year to year? There are several answers to such a question. For one thing, on close examination, the statistics at most schools do not reflect consistent percentages from year to year. There can be wide variations between the number of women in one class and the number in the next, the number of blacks in one class and the number of blacks in the next. Secondly, the students who are admitted are a good reflection of the pool of students who apply. If 30% of the applicants who apply to a medical school are women, you would expect that the proportion of women actually admitted would be somewhere close to 30%. (If you wanted to assert that the 30% of the class who are women had weaker records than the 70% who are men, I think the burden of proof to produce some convincing evidence would be on you.) Finally, all admissions committees value diversity in the classes that they put together, so therefore it is entirely to be expected that there will be various percentages of various types of people in each class. But even white males can use the diversity factor to their advantage, if they construct their applications properly. Admissions officers do not spend their time rejecting applicants because they are of the wrong sex or race, and you as an applicant should not place undue focus on this aspect of the process.

The Wait List (and the Role of Personal Connections)

If you find yourself on a Wait List, you should be aware of several things. Each school has a different conception of what a Wait List is. For some schools, a Wait List is a place for people they want to admit but about whom they are not completely sure; these schools end up taking 90–95% of the applicants from the list each year. Other schools strictly see the Wait List as a safety net in case the school's yield, the percentage of students who accept the school's offer of admission, declines dramatically. For such schools, only 0–10% of the applicants on the Wait List will end up being accepted, and often the number is zero. Finally, the majority of schools probably aim to take a certain number of students from the list each year, anywhere from 10–75%. In these cases, you would have some chance of acceptance off the list, but it would be nowhere close to a certainty. If you find yourself on a Wait List, obviously it behooves you to find out what that particular school's practice is. Many admissions offices are considerate enough to tell you over the phone or through the mail what percentage of its Wait List in recent years has eventually been admitted.

Another thing to be aware of is that most, although certainly not all, schools rank the applicants on the Wait List. Ranking is based on who the admissions committee or the Dean of Admissions thinks is most deserving of admission, not on the order in which applicants are placed on the list; thus the rankings constantly change as new students are added. Obviously, it makes a big difference whether you are 2nd or 98th on a Wait List of 100. Admissions officers are much more reluctant to tell you where you stand on their Wait List, although they occasionally do so (often to the candidate's counsellor rather than to the candidate himself), and it is worth the effort to try to find out. This is one area where personal connections through faculty or alumni of the school involved can be very effective. By having someone make an indirect inquiry to the admissions office on your behalf, you may be better able to find out where you stand.

You should also be aware that your position on the Wait List is not static. Often, applicants are moved up in the rankings, and occasionally applicants are removed from the Wait List entirely and admitted while the rest of the Wait List stays exactly where it is. The cause of such a change would be new information which you supply to the committee. Thus, if you find yourself on a Wait List, the smart thing to do is to launch immediately into a campaign to augment your application. You already know that the school is interested in and seriously considering you; it is quite possible that additional favorable information could decisively tip the scales in your favor.

There are basically three types of new information which you can bring to the attention of the admission committee: new grades, new job experiences or extracurricular activities, and additional recommendations. Clearly, the most influential is excellent new grades (while you are on the Wait List, the school will probably ask you for these itself). Let's say you are a senior in college applying to graduate schools. If you apply in the fall, obviously you will not be applying with the Fall grades for your senior year. If you find yourself on a Wait List in February, and your Fall Grades are at all an improvement on your last year, it is essential that you have them transmitted to the admissions committee. By the same token, if you find yourself on a Wait List in July, you should transmit your spring grades, though again, only if they show improvement.

If you are working, and have a new job experience (either you have switched companies, you have switched positions within a company, or you have been given new assignments or added responsibility at your old position), you should send in a one or two page essay describing it. If you are in school, and have taken on a new extracurricular activity (you've become a leader in an organization, you've taken a new part-time job, or you're engaged in some significant new research), you should send in an essay describing it. Notice that the crucial word here is "new." If your supplemental information describes an activity which you were already engaged in when you filed your original application, the admissions committee is going to wonder why you didn't discuss it the first time. If you merely repeat in greater detail material you have already mentioned in your original application, the admissions committee will not find what you have to say very interesting, and, if anything, your rehash will have a desperate quality which will lower the admissions officers' opinion of you. Make sure you get involved in, and are able to talk about, something new.

If you are on a Wait List, you should have some supplementary recommendations sent. Obviously, the recommendations should be from people who have not written to that particular school previously; I would say two to four new recommendations is the right range. Preferably, one or more should be from people who are dealing with you right now: a current teacher or your current supervisor at work. With a "What-have-you-done-for-me-lately?" attitude, the admissions committee will be interested in what you have been doing recently, your new maturity, and so on. A single new recommendation is unlikely to make much of an impression; more than four and you will look like you are mounting a desperate campaign, an impression you certainly want to avoid. Ideally, the new recommendations should be individual letters (rather than new form recommendations) which look spontaneous: "It has come to my attention that Stanley Smith is on your Wait List. He is an outstanding young man and I wish to urge you to admit him..."

Another factor you should be aware of is that one of the purposes of the Wait List is to test the strength of your desire to attend the school involved. Presumably, during the period in which you are on the Wait List, you will receive acceptances from other schools. If you accept at another school, you will probably take your name off of the Wait List at the first, thus allowing the first school to give your spot to someone else. If you are really interested in the first school, presumably you will hang on to the end. While you are on the Wait List, you are, of course, free to write to that school and express in rhapsodic terms how much you would love to walk through their ivied halls and grovel at the feet of their brilliant professors. This is known as a "Hungry for Harvard" letter. If you decide to write one, and there is no reason why you shouldn't since you have very little to lose, you must be sure to promise specifically that you will attend the school if accepted. Even then, such a letter is unlikely to have much of an effect unless it is unusually eloquent. Note that you should never, ever, in this or any other context in the application process, beg to be admitted. Using the word 'beg' in any way, or otherwise pleading with the admissions committee, is a sign of desperation and will not be favorably received by the committee. A greater effect may be produced if a third party, one of your recommenders, writes and says: "I have spoken to Stanley, and he has repeatedly expressed to me his keen desire to attend your school." Certainly such a letter cannot work miracles, but in conjunction with other new factors it can have an effect.

Yet another strategy in this situation, which can be used in conjunction with your own "Hungry for Harvard" letter and words from your recommender, is what is called an "Impassioned Family Letter." Basically, this involves one of your parents writing to the admissions committee and stating how seriously you want to attend the school in question. Unlike the other strategies mentioned here, the "Impassioned Family Letter" can only be written when you are applying from high school to college; no parental contact in this vein with any graduate school could ever be successful. Both applicants and parents should note that the "Impassioned Family Letter" is the *only* time that direct parental involvement in the admissions process can ever be of any assistance whatsoever.

In addition, an "Impassioned Family Letter" is always a high-risk proposition, with many pitfalls awaiting the unwary: The parent writing the letter should always do so on plain, personal stationery; if he is the President of a corporation or a big-time lawyer, writing on business stationery will be seen by the admissions committee as a form of pressure or pushiness. The admissions committee already knows how prominent he is, or will find out soon enough; he would want to appear modest in his approach. His tone must be completely reasonable, understated, even-handed, and deferential; anything which could be taken as pressure, hysteria, or rudeness will kill the effort. He should never give a list of the applicant's achievements; the admissions committee already knows them from reading the application, and they will either be bored or feel he is being condescending if he repeats them.

Also, at no point in the letter should he begin apologizing or giving alibis for the applicant's weaknesses. Instead, the letter should contain only the following things: emphasize the applicant's maturity; show an understanding of the special aspects of the particular college to which he is writing; and explain why his son or daughter wants to go there, giving specific reasons (note that this is completely different from why *he* wants his son or daughter to go there, why he would want to go there if he had the chance, and if he is an alumnus why he enjoyed going there many years ago). As you can see, the only things which a parent can accomplish from an "Impassioned Family Letter" is to be a witness for the applicant's maturity, and to add credibility to the applicant's assertion that he really wants to go to the particular college involved. Nothing more can be accomplished, and thus, absolutely nothing more should be written.

The final thing you as an applicant on a Wait List can do is to request an interview to allow you to plead your case in person. Most schools have a rule against interviewing candidates while they are on the Wait List, the theory being that a person who gets such an interview will gain a significant advantage over others on the Wait List who do not. This theory is absolutely sound, and therefore, if you interview well, you should by all means request one. If the school grants interviews to candidates on the Wait List, or will grant you an exception to their general rule, you should try to accomplish three things during that interview: (1) since you were put on the Wait List, the admissions committee perceived some weakness in your record, probably in your academic record; try to draw out of your interviewer what that weakness might be, and then present some arguments to dispel the doubt; (2) update your file by telling the interviewer about the interesting things you have been doing since you wrote the application; and (3) strongly express your enthusiasm for and knowledge of the school, and tell the interviewer that you would attend if accepted.

You should also know that the Wait List is the area in which the Dean of Admissions and the admissions committee can exercise their greatest discretion. You have already been certified as qualified for the school, since otherwise you would have been rejected outright and never appeared on the Wait List; the admissions committee as a whole has already reviewed your file and given you partial approval. Thus, at a school where Wait List candidates do not have to be reviewed anew by the full admissions committee, if the dean admits you he is not bypassing the committee; he will simply be admitting you pursuant to a previous vote of approval, albeit qualified, by the committee.

What this means in practical terms is that the Wait List stage is the time in which personal influence, friendships with members of the admissions committee, and alumni connections become most important. Obviously, the effectiveness of any such campaign will vary widely from school to school. Small private colleges are clearly the most susceptible to influence. Such colleges are constantly short of funds and, thus, significantly at the mercy of their alumni donors. The trick in that situation is to avoid appearing so heavy-handed in your approach that your acceptance becomes a moral issue for the admissions committee and the college. If forced into such a position, the college will usually do the honorable thing and tell both you and your alumni allies to go to hell. The proper approach is to do everything to remain gentle and reasonable, and to aim at persuading the Dean of Admissions to see what a fine person the candidate is. The focus should always be on the candidate, not on the force of the influence.

Large public universities are usually not influenced by alumni opinion unless the alumnus involved is a particularly heavy donor or involved in football recruiting. They are sometimes susceptible to persuasion by political figures, however, especially state legislators who have control over appropriations for the university, with whom the school wants to remain friendly. Universities with the highest academic reputations and huge endowments, such as Harvard and Yale, are virtually immune to raw pressure. (Harvard, for example, routinely turns down applications from sons and daughters of its trustees and overseers.) The only approach with this type of school which has a chance of being successful is via people who, through personal friendships or academic reputation, have some special credibility with members of the admissions committee or other very prominent members of the faculty. If someone with experience and a track record in recommending people to the school knows you well and is willing to put his or her credibility on the line for you, then there may be a chance that you can be admitted from the Wait List as a result. (Note that this is very different from being moved from the Definite Reject category to admission, or even from the Average/Borderline category to admission.)

Also, when dealing with such institutions, this is one instance in life where "going straight to the top" is definitely the wrong strategy. Derek Bok and A. Bartlett Giamatti, the Presidents of Harvard and Yale, respectively, probably get a hundred requests a year each to intervene in admissions decisions. If they were to do so even once, they would undermine completely the independence of their admissions committees and rearrange the political scenery on campus. Therefore, to my knowledge at least, wisely they never intervene. The best strategy is to have the pitch urging your admission from the Wait List come indirectly, rather than through the university's chain of command. The success of any effort to use personal or family influence to gain acceptance off the Wait List in every case will depend a great deal upon the experience and political independence of the Dean of Admissions. Some deans are so firmly entrenched that no one could ever hope to influence them. Others probably have the backbone of a banana. This is the type of thing you will have to investigate on a school-by-school basis.

One precaution you should always take if you find yourself on a Wait List is to communicate with the school once a month or so to keep them apprised of your interest. This is not the same as making a pest of yourself; you should not call the Dean of Admissions and try to engage him in conversation once a month. What you should do is either call an underling, or write a routine letter (some schools even supply form postcards for this purpose), once a month expressing your continued strong interest in being admitted. The danger of not doing so is vividly illustrated by the following true story.

□**Case History #2:** Tony Samson was a senior at Harvard College and had compiled a brilliant record both overall and in his pre-medical courses. He wanted to be a doctor, and applied to Harvard and Yale medical schools, among others. He was accepted by Yale and put on Harvard's Wait List in the fall. In April, out of the blue, he received the following letter from the Harvard Medical School's admissions office: "Dear Mr. Samson, Thank you for informing us that you wish to be taken off our Wait List. We appreciate your notifying us, as we can now offer your spot to another qualified applicant." Tony was absolutely outraged, and immediately called the Dean of Admissions at the school. As it turned out, the Medical School had received a letter asking that Tony be taken off the Wait List, with a forgery of Tony's signature at the end. Had it not been for Harvard's practice of sending out a routine confirmation letter, Tony might not have discovered the fraudulent letter until the end of the summer, if ever, at which time it might have been too late. As it turned out, Tony was first on Harvard's Wait List, and, in fact, he was soon accepted. The forger was discovered to be another pre-med in Tony's house, who had been turned down at Harvard and wanted to spoil it for someone else. The forger was expelled from Harvard College just weeks before he was to have graduated, and his acceptances at other medical schools were withdrawn by those schools.

Although this is the most extreme example of what could happen to you on a Wait List, it illustrates the importance of keeping in contact with the admissions committee so that your file is not lost in the shuffle.

Something else to keep in the back of your mind is that many schools, especially colleges, have what is called a "Courtesy Wait List." What this means is that the school, instead of rejecting the candidate outright early in the season, will put him on the Wait List as a "courtesy," with the intent of rejecting him later in the season. The Courtesy Wait List is used primarily with legacies (children of alumni), candidates from prep schools applying to private colleges, and candidates who seem to have active alumni support, but who for one reason or another do not make the grade. The Courtesy Wait List could mean that the candidates are added to the regular Wait List, only at the very bottom, or it could mean a separate Wait List altogether. In either event, the rationale is to allow Johnny (and Johnny's parents) to tell the world that he was "Waitlisted" at Brown rather than "Rejected." In another way it is quite unfair, since inevitably it raises false hopes in the candidate, and there is no way to tell (without inside information from the admissions office) whether one is on the real Wait List or the Courtesy Wait List. With enough alumni pressure it may be possible to be admitted from the Courtesy Wait List, but undoubtedly it is very rare.

Finally, you should realize that a main feature of being on the Wait List is simply waiting. As noted before, the Wait List is, in part, a test by the school to see how long you are willing to wait, an indication of how badly you want to go to their school. Some Wait Lists have been known to be open into August for a term starting in September; in one case I know of, someone was accepted off of a Wait List ten days after the term had opened (he had wisely gone to another school by then). Be aware that the longer you remain on the list, the more your chances improve. Other people are continually signing on with other schools and dropping off the list. If you find yourself on a Wait List of a school to which you very much want to go, you should immediately send your new information to the school, and then hang on for the ride.

Getting in Through the Back Door: Some Alternate Strategies

If you have identified a particular school you desperately want to go to, and have either assessed your chances of acceptance as slim, or have already been rejected, there is always the "back door" alternative. The successful back door approach varies from school to school, so you will have to do some careful research.

If you have already been rejected, you can appeal the decision. The key ingredient in a successful appeal is *always* new information. If you appeal with the exact same file, you will get the exact same rejection letter. A very few schools, like the University of California, have a formal appeal system; at such schools an appeal may be successful if you present good new information. At other schools, appeals will be handled on a "case-by-case" basis, which in practical terms means that the admissions office will rally to protect its initial decision, and your chances are just about zero unless you present amazing new information, or unless there was a serious miscarriage of justice.

Another option is to sue in court, claiming that some unfairness in the system caused your rejection. This is almost inevitably an extremely bad idea, and you should put it out of your mind. It is very difficult to prove some serious unfairness, and it is even more difficult to show that that unfairness caused your rejection. Any such litigation would be extremely expensive, as well. And finally, you should learn from the experiences of others: The two students who have sued and won, Marco DeFunis, Jr. and Allan Bakke, are marked men. Whatever they do in life, whatever success they achieve in their professions, will be overshadowed by the court cases which bear their name. They will be haunted by a political issue greater than they are. That is a heavy price to pay to go to some school for three or four years.

A third option is to apply again during the next admissions season. This is seldom successful. (Note the discussion of holdovers in the preceding Timing section.) It is true that admissions standards at a school may vary somewhat from year to year; you may be rejected in a tough year and accepted in an easy year. Or you may have been rejected when you applied late in the season, but might be accepted if you applied on October 1st. Unfortunately, there are a number of fallacies in these arguments. You have no idea whether the next year will be an easy year, or even harder. You probably have no idea whether you were a very firm reject, or right on the borderline. And finally, there is the aspect of human nature you cannot fight: An admissions committee will tend to validate decisions it has made previously. Again, as with appeals, your only hope is through significant new information. You *must* put the interim year to extremely good use, and be able to present a thoroughly revised application. (Business School deferrals are a completely different subject, and are discussed below.)

If you want to get into a particular college, a frequent strategy is to go to that university's summer school while you are still in high school. This strategy is overrated; the number of students for whom it has worked is far fewer than the number for whom it has failed. If you are determined to try this route, there are several things you must do in order to make it effective: take difficult courses; take a heavy course load, two courses instead of just one; make sure your courses are taught by full professors at that university, not graduate students and not visiting professors from some other university (who will not be nearly as helpful in recommending you); and make sure you get A's and get to know your professors well, so that they can write you sterling recommendations. Nothing will seal your fate more quickly when applying to Cornell than to have a B− or a C from the Cornell Summer School.

If you want to get into a graduate school through a back door, the strategies become more subtle. One approach is to apply to an easy school in the university, do very well there for a semester or two, then "discover" that you are really suited for some other profession, and either transfer to the more difficult school or take up a joint degree. For example, you might enter the Columbia School of International Affairs (which is relatively easy to be admitted to), and then transfer to or take a joint degree with the Columbia Business School. I know of at least one student who went to the Kennedy School of Government at Harvard (a school which is extremely easy to enter), did very well there for two years, and then on that basis was admitted to Harvard Law School, where he would not have had a chance to be admitted originally. Clearly, if you have performed at an A level at one graduate school in a university, the other graduate school in the same university will be hard-pressed to challenge your intellectual achievements, and your chances for admission will improve dramatically. But this gambit is not foolproof, especially if your reasons for transferring seem insincere; and you must also be aware of the possibility that you will not gain the A record needed—you must weigh the cost of a year of your life spent on a strategy which may not succeed.

Another strategy is little-known but can be very effective. Some, though certainly not all, graduate schools operate on trimester and quarter systems, and accept students not only for classes which start in the fall but also ones which start in the spring and summer. At some of these schools, the standards of admission for the spring and summer groups are significantly lower than for the fall. (The schools do not, of course, announce this, and will probably deny it for the record. But the real statistics often show otherwise.) If you are willing to start graduate school at an odd time of year, applying during the off-season may be an excellent way to beat the crowds and be considered with a group which has less competition per available seat and whose applicants may have considerably weaker records. In the admissions game, being in the right place at the right time can make all the difference in the world.

CHAPTER 2
Factors in the Admissions Decision

As noted earlier, the first step in virtually every admissions process is to place applicants into three or more categories based more or less entirely on the academic credentials of grades and test scores. Depending on the school involved, this process can choose anywhere from 15% to 80% of a class. The remaining candidates are placed in the Average/Borderline category (not counting the Definite Rejects). You should always keep in mind that not everyone in this category is considered equal; in fact, academic credentials still remain the most important factor in selecting from the Average/Borderline pool. Fortunately, however, many other factors also come into play.

By the Numbers: An Overview

Before an examination of all of the different non-numerical factors, you should be aware that different types of schools value different types of activities differently. Also, each school has its own priorities and practices, some of which differ from the norm. Unfortunately, no one can say what the admissions officers of every school in the country are looking for. (What does Stanford Business School look for as opposed to the University of Chicago Law School as against Oberlin College, etc.? No one has that much information, especially since a great deal of it becomes outdated each year.) It is, however, possible to identify general trends, to deduce from the schools' actual behavior what their priorities are. Please note that the following percentages are not based on university propaganda. Every school whose catalog you will ever read, every admissions officer to whom you will ever talk, will tell you until they are blue in the face about how they make every effort to see the whole person, and how it is impossible to quantify their decision-making process. *This is hogwash.* What it really means is either they don't want to tell you, since it fuels a complaint that you were treated differently (and thus unfairly) if you are rejected, or they have never sat down and taken a good hard look at what really counts in their decision-making process.

A final limitation of the chart below is that it only applies to 90% of the applicant pool, and not to special cases such as disadvantaged minorities, Vietnam veterans, exceptional athletes, and so on. Special cases, which will be discussed in greater depth below, are handled separately in the minds of admissions officers, and decisions about them focus on very different questions unrelated to this scale.

So remember the limitations: The chart only applies to ordinary applicants who are already in the Average/Borderline category, and for an individual school the chart could differ markedly:

	Colleges	Law Schools	Business Schools	Arts & Science Graduate Schools	Medical Schools
Grades (GPA)	30%	45%	25%[1]	60%	55%
Standardized Test Scores	20	43	20	20	25
Work Experience	2	2	28[2]	1	4[3]
Application & Essay	12	4	20	6	4
Extracurricular Activities	10	3	3	2	2
Interview	6	0	0	0	8
Recommendations	18	2	3	10	2
Other[4]	2	1	1	1	0
Total Nonacademic	50	12	55	20	20

All numbers are percentages.

1. Becomes less important once you are more than five years out of college.
2. The quality of your experience, as expressed in your essay, is crucial here.
3. Must be related to medicine in order to be relevant.
4. Includes alumni connections, regional diversity, etc.

Several quick conclusions can be reached from this chart:

■ There is no substitute for good grades. If you have excellent grades, your chances will always be good despite weaknesses in other areas.
■ The "Tyranny of Standardized Testing" is simply not a fact. Good test

scores certainly help, but there are plenty of ways to get in without them.

- Work experience, either part-time or full-time, is rarely going to be a major factor. The academy remains skeptical of the real world.
- Extracurricular and community activities are very important for getting into college, but much less relevant later unless they are extraordinary.
- Recommendations are generally only critical for colleges and arts and sciences graduate schools.

The Unique versus the Well-Rounded

One of the most consistent myths about admission to college, and to a lesser extent graduate schools, is that admissions committees look for well-rounded individuals, miniature Renaissance men. This may have been true before World War II, when higher education was the province of the rich and the upper middle class, but it is certainly not true today. It is, of course, possible to be admitted to a top college because you are well-rounded, but it is no longer a necessity.

The actual way admissions committees choose from their candidate pools is to mix together all the above factors for each candidate and see what comes out. There are four common scenarios:

1. The Single Overwhelmingly Positive Factor: You have successfully overcome a significant disadvantage or handicap. You have made an extraordinary contribution to the community. You have had an extraordinary academic triumph, such as making an original scientific discovery or publication of a serious, scholarly book. For a college applicant, you have demonstrated outstanding talent in some field of the arts or in athletics. A distinguished scholar who is well known to or friends with members of the admissions committee gives you his highest endorsement.

2. The Cumulative Effect of a Large Number of Positive Factors: You did well while taking a difficult course load and you worked part-time while in school to finance your education and you played a significant leadership role in one or two extracurricular or community activities and you turned in a well-written and interesting application and your recommendations are all extremely favorable. Although you do not necessarily need every one of these ingredients, note that you definitely do need several.

3. The Cumulative Effect of Several Negative Factors: Your GPA was based on an undemanding curriculum, and you have listed membership in many extracurricular organizations but you were a leader in none, and your application is sloppy, or it is poorly written, or it is well-written but a pile of mush, and you didn't hit it off with your interviewer, and one of your recommendations is slightly on the lukewarm side. Notice that none of these factors is particularly significant alone, but the cumulative effect can be devastating.

4. The Single Overwhelming Negative Factor: The admissions committee discovers a lie in your application. You have a mediocre GPA and the admissions committee sees that you took a light course load. You are applying to graduate school several years out of college, and you fail to account for some of the years in the interim. You have no extracurricular or community activities at all (and you are not an academic genius). Your application shows that you have significant difficulty writing coherent English. You say something offensive in your application, either about the school, or about some group or class of people. You come off in your application as immature. You come off in your application as arrogant or pompous (and again, you are not an academic genius). One or more of your recommendations says something negative about you.

These are the four typical cases. Obviously there are instances which fall between any two of the cases, and there are instances where two are combined (for example, a student who has an excellent overall record and who also has some extraordinary quality).

What specific things do admissions officers consider important? It is impossible to produce a completely exhaustive list, since from time to time applicants come along with some extremely unusual qualities or experiences which add to the list. With the thought in mind that you should always be looking to come up with something really new, here is a catalog of the standard items. Remember that admissions committees differ widely in their appraisal of the importance of each factor.

Grades: Quantity and Quality

The basic number is, of course, your Grade Point Average or GPA. Please note that in applying to virtually every graduate school, your grades must be converted to a 4.0 scale. If you are applying to law school, this will be done for you by LSDAS (Law School Data Assembly Services). Check their work to make sure they have done so correctly. Note that the LSDAS system has some quirks. For one, they round all letter grades to the nearest full grade; thus, a B+ becomes a B, while an A− becomes an A. This discriminates against the student with many B+'s and for the student with many A−'s. (The rich get richer.) If you are applying to other types of graduate schools, and you have attended a place like Rutgers which has an anachronistic grading system off the 4.0 scale, you may be given an opportunity to do the conversion yourself. Please be aware that there is a certain amount of creativity involved in making such a conversion (witness LSDAS's odd system). You do not necessarily have to accept the standard method used by the school you attended, so long as the system you use is rational, and so long as you explain to the school to which you are applying how you made the conversion.

Creativity also comes into play in the rounding off process, once you have calculated your GPA to the twelfth decimal place. Isn't a 3.7569 really a 3.8?

Virtually every college is aware that an A − average from Exeter is not the same as an A − from Des Moines Senior High School. Virtually every graduate school is aware that a 3.75 from Cal Tech or Smith is not the same as a 3.75 from the University of Alabama or Simmons. There is no question that some schools demand more and significantly harder work from their students (usually a reflection of the intellectual integrity of the institution and the caliber of student they can attract), and that some schools have significantly tougher grading scales than others. The latter is usually the result of some decision by a long-forgotten dean, perpetuated by institutional inertia. For example, Boston University Law School grades on a 0−100 scale, but only a handful of students receive a 90 or above in even a single course. Does this make B.U. a great law school? Certainly not. Is there any rational reason for it? No. Does it hurt the average B.U. law student when he looks for a job outside of Massachusetts? Probably. The question is, how do schools to which you will be applying factor this sort of information into their decisions? Virtually none disregard it entirely. A few, very few, actually make a list of all the schools which send them candidates, rank the schools, and then place a numerical value on each. The numerical value is either multiplied by the GPA, as in the GPA's of all candidates from Smith will be multiplied by 1.10, increasing them by 10%, or added to the GPA, as in the GPA's of all candidates from Stanford will have 0.15 points added to them, so that a 3.30 GPA becomes a 3.45 when compared with other schools. On the whole, however, admissions officers are wary of this type of exactitude (somewhat ironic in view of the reliance of many on numerical cut-offs), and very few schools actually use such formulas.

The main practice is much less systematic. As a file is being passed around at the admissions committee meeting, someone will remark that the candidate should be given the benefit of the doubt (or should not be given the benefit of the doubt) based on what school the candidate went to; or someone will remark that in recent years the committee has consistently taken people who had over a 3.2 from the candidate's school and they have all been successful students. How much weight this sort of comment will carry can vary greatly from case to case. If the committee is leaning toward the candidate, this may tip the scales decisively in his favor; if the committee is tending negatively, it is quite unlikely to turn the tide. As a general rule, there is no question that graduates of major preparatory schools have a significantly improved chance of getting into selective colleges, and graduates of Ivy League and Seven Sister colleges have a significantly better chance to get into top graduate schools nationwide. (At one time some prep schools were consistent feeder schools to particular colleges, veritable farm teams. The Lawrenceville School in New Jersey, for example, once sent over 50% of its graduating classes to Princeton. Those days are, however, gone forever.) The basic reason is that these schools have long, documented track records of producing a high percentage of able students, and those institutional track records cannot help but rub off on individual candidates.

The good news is that I think it is safe to say that few admissions committees actively discriminate against candidates from schools they consider weak. In order to be taken seriously from such a school, you will need an A or close to an A average, but after that you are on your own. By schools which are considered weak, I am referring to small, obscure schools; schools which have been founded recently and do not have established reputations; local branches of a state university which do not share the reputation of the flagship university; community colleges; religious schools which are viewed as down-playing academics; and schools which have a reputation as "party schools." It is probably extremely rare, if not unknown, for someone to be denied admission solely because of the school he attended; on the other hand, the burden of proof is going to be on that person to demonstrate a lot of other positive characteristics.

Finally, if you come from a small school, or if you are applying to schools in a different region of the country, or, especially, if you are applying from abroad, it is a serious mistake to assume that the admissions committee will be aware of the good reputation of your school. Members of admissions committees are human beings; usually only a few are full-time admissions officers. Very few admissions officers are walking encyclopedias of information about every school in the country. Sometimes what passes for information is outdated or is simply rumor, hearsay, or speculation. This is especially true when applying from high school to college. Most college admissions officers know the amount of work required at the Bronx High School of Science, but most have either never heard of the great majority of high schools in the nation or have only a bare minimum of knowledge. At the graduate school level, if you are applying from a major college, you should have little trouble. But if you are applying from a small college which only sends one student every five years to the graduate school you want to go to, then you may have a problem. Therefore, you need to alert the admissions committee to the rigor of your education.

Most applications have a question somewhere which allows you to comment on your grades. Rather than whining about the C you got your sophomore year because the teacher hated you, you should stress the positive. If your school is obscure, comment on its good reputation locally. (It is a mistake to do this if your school is well known. If you went to Yale College, talking about its good reputation in a graduate school application is likely to be perceived as very arrogant.) More importantly, comment on how rigorous an education you received, with examples. If it's a high school, talk about difficult books you had to read, how many AP courses you took, sophisticated science experiments you did, etc. If it's a college, talk about the many advanced courses you were able to take in your major, the difficulty of seminar papers or your thesis, the famous professors you were able to study with, etc. If your school has a reputation as being easy, acknowledge it, and explain how you got a rigorous education in spite of the reputation. Again, do not take for granted that the admissions committee will somehow discover this by looking at your transcript or by some act of divine inspiration.

If admissions committees have difficulty assessing the importance of the reputation of your school when looking at your application, they do even worse in assessing your course load. (This entire section applies only to college students applying to graduate schools. The exact reverse is true for high school students applying to college. See the chapter of applying to college below.) Anyone who has gone to school knows that a large factor in a GPA is course selection. There are innumerable ways to inflate a GPA at any school:

- Take courses anywhere in the school which are considered "guts;"(easy courses);
- Avoid any professor who is stingy with A's;
- Select your major based on its grading practices;
- Take introductory survey courses as a junior or senior;
- Take small seminars where A's are more plentiful;
- If pre-med, take biochemistry in summer school;
- Take easy introductory math courses when you are good at math or have already covered the material in high school;
- Take easy, introductory language courses when you already know the language;
- Cross-register to take courses at a weaker school in your area;
- Cross-register in less demanding divisions of your university;
- Take the minimum number of courses needed to graduate;
- Take pass/fail any courses which might jeopardize your GPA;
- Take courses where homework counts and extra-credit projects are allowed.

If you do these things consistently (without overdoing any one of them, like taking too many courses pass/fail), you may not get the world's greatest education, but your GPA should be bloated to the maximum extent possible. And, unless one of four problems comes up, the schools to which you apply will never know.

Again, the problem the graduate schools have is lack of concrete knowledge. There are hundreds of colleges in the United States, each of which has several dozen majors, hundreds of professors, and hundreds if not thousands of courses. No admissions officer could ever hope to gather enough information to decide whether a candidate's GPA inflates or understates his real ability. Admissions officers' days are too busy with other things for them to gather the huge amounts of data that would be required. The admissions officer's rationalization is that on average the hard courses even out with the easy ones, and this is probably true in most cases, unless you consciously and deliberately set out to inflate your average.

The four situations in which you will have a problem are as follows:

1. You take a gut so notorious that word has spread to the admissions committee you are applying to. At Harvard College, for example, two courses are given in the history department which cover the age of seafaring discovery and conquest. They are known affectionately as *Boats I* and *Boats II*, and they are known to the admissions committees of virtually every major graduate school. Since admissions committees completely miss 99% of all guts on applicants' transcripts, when they finally spot one they may tend to overreact and allow that one course to taint their view of the rest of the transcript. Therefore, courses like this should be avoided at all costs; resist the temptation. Fortunately, such nationally-known or clearly-advertised guts are extremely rare, and probably do not even exist at most colleges.

2. Your major is believed to be a gut major. Some majors are known to be guts virtually everywhere. Physical education is the best example; communications and sociology are so considered by many people. Sometimes gut majors can be pinpointed at particular schools: History is considered soft at some schools, as is geology, but they are not considered so nationwide. Folklore and Mythology, as another example, is considered a soft major at Harvard. I would be going too far to say flatly that such a major should be avoided. But if you choose one the burden of proof shifts to you insofar as the admissions committee is concerned: You must have excellent grades in your courses in that major, and describe in your essays how you personally received a rigorous education, the reputation of your major notwithstanding.

3. You are applying to a graduate school at the same university where you went to college (for example, applying from Notre Dame College to Notre Dame Law School). Your college transcript will come under an intense scrutiny, in obvious distinction from applications from graduates of other colleges. Several factors will be different: The graduate school is likely to have some respect for the intellectual caliber of the undergraduate college, especially since the graduate school will take many students each year from the college. (Harvard College sends more students to Harvard Law School, Harvard Business School, and Harvard Medical School than any other college each year, usually more than double the next rival.) Thus no sales pitch is needed on the subject of what a fine school you go to. The graduate school is likely to have a formal or informal quota for its undergraduate college. Consequently, there will be more head-to-head comparison with other candidates from your undergraduate school. The possible presence of a quota emphasizes the importance of filing an early application. Finally, when you apply to another school within the same university, you must assume that all guts will be easily discovered. They will either be known to the graduate school admissions committee, or will be uncovered with a quick phone call.

4. The last situation, and the most difficult to protect against, is when one of the people writing a recommendation for you qualifies your accomplishments by saying, for example, "Patty is a very intelligent student who received excellent grades here, although her curriculum was something less than demanding." An admissions committee would be likely to pay very close attention to such a statement, and would consider it highly unfavorable.

Schools are interested in the trend of grades, not just the actual grades themselves. A weak freshman year can be almost completely wiped out by good upperclass years. A rising trend is viewed very favorably. By the same token, a record which starts strong and then falters is viewed unfavorably, and the GPA is discounted. Whenever there is a favorable trend, it is crucial that the applicant bring it to the attention of the admissions committee. Otherwise the progress may get lost in the shuffle.

One or two poor grades will not seriously mar an otherwise top-flight resume. Again, the burden is on the candidate to explain the weak grades to the committee. "If an otherwise top record combines with 10 credits of D or F in an exceptionally difficult subject area to produce a middle GPA, we try to take that into account."—University of Wisconsin Law School.

Pass/fail courses do not hurt a record at all (assuming you passed), so long as there are not too many. "If only a few courses are taken pass-fail, no serious problem is posed."—Boston College Law School.

However, schools which offer a pass/fail option for an entire course of study, or schools which have only narrative evaluations and no grades, such as Antioch College, pose a special problem. The consensus of graduate schools seems to be that graduates of such programs are at a slight overall disadvantage, and that standardized test scores largely fill the vacuum left by the absence of grades. "Where an applicant has completed substantially all of his or her work in pass-fail, it will probably be necessary for [that] applicant to achieve a superior score on [the LSAT] to have a good chance for admission."—Boston College Law School.

If your grades during one semester were markedly different than your overall average, perhaps because of personal problems or special commitments, those circumstances should be pointed out to the committee. If you changed majors during your college career and had a significantly better record in the new major, this should be pointed out and explained to the committee.

A good number of students, somewhere between college and law school or business school or medical school, pick up a Master's Degree along the way. Candidates invariably place great stock in that degree; they believe it gives the holder some added prestige; they usually get very high grades in the Master's program, and believe that those grades should count heavily, often to cancel out a weaker college record. In actual fact, professional graduate schools almost entirely disregard such degrees and the grades which created them. The reasons have been very well articulated by the University of Washington Law School:

> Many applicants who have been out of undergraduate school for some period report some quantum of part-time graduate study. The Committee seldom makes an adjustment in predicted first year average ranking [and thus admission] for such work on several grounds: (1) such work, particularly in the early part of Masters' degree programs, tend to retrace upper division undergraduate work for the benefit of students new to the graduate school; (2) grades on such work tends to be confined to A's and B's rather than distributed over the broader range of undergraduate grades; and (3) where the work is part-time, we are uncertain as to the effective time demands on the student and thus can not easily compare the grades with those of a full-time student.

So do not expect any bonus at all for such graduate work, unless your college days were more than ten years ago, and your graduate school grades are used to give evidence that you can still do academic work. Incidentally, if you have achieved a Ph.D., professional graduate schools tend to have an entirely different attitude, and will often be quite willing to admit you if you give a coherent reason for wanting to change careers.

A question often asked is whether any particular majors or any particular courses will pave the way to graduate school. With the exception of required pre-medical courses, the answer is a very resounding no. No course of study can adequately prepare you for graduate study, nor should any directly try to do so either. The best course of study for law school is probably mathematics and philosophy, since they both teach habits of clear thinking, but both are as far from the subject matter of law as can be imagined. "It is perhaps advisable, however, for the prospective law students to avoid undergraduate courses in law designed to prepare one for other callings as they may duplicate law school work. Ordinarily, the time and effort are better spent studying other fields."—Northwestern Law School.

In forming an application strategy, however, some majors are, indeed, better than others. Basically, your choice of major can help make you an interesting person to the admissions committee. If you major in something really obscure like Egyptology, or even something moderately unusual like Italian literature, or classics or philosophy, you will stand out from the herd of economics and political science majors applying to business schools and law schools—or from the biology and biochemistry majors flooding medical schools. It is certainly true that more political science majors go to law school each fall, but by percentages accepted, I would say philosophy majors are ahead. The choice of a major as an undergraduate allows you to find a field which will give you a diversity edge, as long as you have a real interest in the field as well.

A final area which should be noted is rank in class. Colleges often consider rank in class quite important when choosing among high school students. This is especially true for applicants from high schools which are not well known; rank in class can tell the college whether a B + average is very good or simply the result of grade inflation. Few graduate schools consider rank in class as an item worthy of consideration apart from grades. However, it may be used as a device to measure grade inflation at the particular school you attended.

"The Tyranny of Testing"

Much is made of the importance of standardized testing to the admissions process. But as the chart provided earlier shows, although the tests—the SAT, the LSAT, the GMAT, the GRE, and the MCAT—are important, they are not all-powerful. The major benefit the tests provide is that they are the great leveler; they provide a uniform, nationwide basis of comparison. They are particularly helpful to students who go to obscure high schools or colleges in obscure parts of the country; a very high test score will help such a person be noticed by major universities, when otherwise he would have stood little chance.

Why do colleges and graduate schools use the tests? Basically they are used to predict grades. For colleges, to predict the first year or two; for graduate schools, the first year. If, for example, a law school gives the Educational Testing Service statistical data for a number of previous years, including LSAT scores, college GPA, and first-year law grades, ETS will produce a statistical study for that law school showing what combination of college grades and test scores would have predicted, on average, the students' first year grades. (ETS does this free as a service to the law schools, in order to promote its tests, of course.) ETS will produce for each school a historical weighting of the two factors (for example, grades 60% and LSAT 40%) which would do the best job of predicting first year grades. Most law schools use

ETS's numbers extensively; ETS will compute an "Index Number" for each student based on the schools weighting, and thus the school can exactly rank each student. The admissions process is then based on that index.

Law schools have the most formal system; most other schools merely use the standardized test as a normal factor in the admissions process. Virtually every school requires some sort of standardized test; Bowdoin is the only major college in the country which does not require them for admission.

There are two procedural matters of importance: Many test-takers are concerned about what happens when they are sick the day of the test and elect to take it anyway. If you feel you did poorly, you can cancel the scoring of your exam; your exam will be destroyed and never scored. The slight disadvantage this entails is that the schools to which you are applying will be informed that you were exposed to an exam but cancelled your score; the schools may discount your next score since it will be the second time for you. It is unlikely that this will be much of a factor, however. Your other option is to let the score stand and, if you are dissatisfied, write to the schools to which you are applying and tell them how sick you were that day. Schools get letters like this quite often; in order for the excuse to be credible, however, you must leave a paper trail. Under ETS procedures, what you must do is inform the ETS supervisor at the test site about your illness. He will enter it into the official log for the exam. ETS can then document that you were, in fact ill, and then your letter will be taken seriously.

The second procedural point is simpler. Many test-takers wonder what will happen if they take an exam more than once. The official ETS recommendation is that schools receiving the scores should average them. Virtually all schools will do this unless there is a claim of illness, or unless one score is several years older than the other, in which case the more recent score will receive more weight.

Some applicants feel that standardized tests consistently under-represent their abilities. If you have done poorly on such an exam, and have consistently done poorly on such exams, *and* you otherwise have an outstanding academic record, it may be worth your while to make such a claim to schools to which you are applying. The key ingredient, however, is that you must supply lots of documented evidence. "Candidates sometimes seek to establish that their academic potential is not reflected by scores on standardized tests. If you claim this to be true in your case, please attach appropriate documentation (e.g., SAT scores)."—University of Texas Law School.

Finally, the great question is, does coaching work? The answer, despite ETS's propaganda on the subject, is clearly an unequivocally yes. The first witness will be Dr. John A. Winterbottom, then director of graduate and professional school testing programs at ETS. He testified in the trial of *DeFunis v. Odegaard*, the first educational reverse discrimination case. Note that he is on the witness stand, and thus sworn to tell the truth: "When...the [LSAT] is taken for a second time, another element comes into the picture...which we cannot measure, and to which we refer as practice effect. This...stems from the fact that...the candidate has gained a certain familiarity with the test....He does not know exactly what kind of questions will be on it the second time, but he knows their general structure. He knows better how to go about attacking them. There is no question about it that the test score on the second testing will go up by some undeterminable amount for each candidate as a result of that practice effect....[T]he situation usually is that the first score, particularly if the candidate has been feeling unwell when he took it, or excessively anxious, is likely to be somewhat of an underestimate of his true ability. The second score, as a result of this practice effect, is likely to be something of an overestimate of his true ability...."

Since a practice effect exists, I think a rational person would take a test preparation course, get most if not all of the value of the practice effect there, and then go into the test prepared and get a score which would be an "overestimate" of one's true ability. What an ideal position to be in; one has all schools overestimating one's ability!

In addition, ETS's claim that its tests are not coachable is patently false. It is true that some sections are more coachable than others, but some are extremely difficult without coaching and quite easy with it. Later in his testimony, Dr. Winterbottom said that one in one hundred people who takes the test a second time scores a gain of 175 points. This is an absolutely enormous gain; from a 550 to 725 is a huge jump. If such jumps are not only possible, but occur as often as 1 in 100 times, then coaching would seem to be exactly the right thing to help the test-taker up that path.

Personal Qualities

As you think about the personal qualities of candidates which are important in admissions decisions, put yourself in the shoes of the admissions officer for a moment. What would you be looking for? What kind of questions would you ask yourself about the candidates you see? The first question is always, Can this person handle the work? But once that is answered in the affirmative, a number of others become important. Is this person mature and conscientious enough to do well at our school? Is this person insecure? Immature? Does this person care about other people? Will this person bring credit to our school in the future? These questions will underlie much of the remaining factors.

Work Experience: Character and the Will to Learn

Work experience while in high school and college can be used for two very different purposes. The first is to establish your interest in and knowledge of a particular field. You want to be a lawyer, so you work as a paralegal during college. You want to be a doctor, so you work in a lab. Such a use of work experience only has a very minor effect on admissions decisions. In most cases, you could just as easily be accepted without any such experiences. To understand how prevalent some type of work experience or extracurricular experience is, consider the following statistics reported by Cornell Law School: in a recent class, 43% had held a full-time job before entering law school; 44% had held a law-related job before entering law school; 41% had been involved in student government; 25% had been editors or reporters for their college newspapers; 19% had been varsity athletes in college; 13% had done some graduate work before law school; and 19% had studied abroad before law school. To have done something other than straight studying is thus quite common; the task is to make what you have done sound unusually interesting to the admissions committee.

The second use of work experience is that it shows character. For this, the work experience need not be in a particular field; virtually anything will do. In fact, the more blue collar the job, the more vivid an impression you can weave out of it. The basic purpose of work experience here is to show that you were so determined to fight for an education that you were willing to take on any job to help pay your way through. Again, admissions committees are interested in diversity and they are interested in helping the disadvantaged; if you were a cab driver or a farm worker or a manual laborer to help pay for your education, you have become your own best character witness. The more dramatic you can make your triumph over poverty and hardship, the more your chances improve.

A particularly good type of work experience is military service. All schools are under a governmental mandate to find and accept more qualified servicemen, especially from the Vietnam era. And most admissions committees should recognize the special service contribution of someone who served honorably in the armed forces (just as they recognized someone who served in the Peace Corps, or taught in an inner-city school, for example). As with other jobs, you should describe in specific detail what your functions in the service were, and you should explain how your experiences caused you to want to seek further education. Finally, if you were an officer, you probably have some advantage when applying to business schools; major business schools have traditionally taken a good number of their students directly from the military, since many officers have a considerable degree of management experience in the service. You should use the experience you have gained in the military to your full advantage in applying to schools.

Your Application and Essay

Specific parts of the application and essay will be dealt with below, and thus will not be mentioned here. The application and the essay are always important aspects of your admission package, and even more importantly, they are almost completely in your hands. Be sure you use them to the full extent possible.

An important subject for you to keep in mind when thinking about the essay is the importance of always staying within the truth. It is very important that you be creative in your application and squeeze the most amount of value out of every experience you have had. It is another thing entirely to fabricate information about yourself. Discovery of the fabrication will lead to automatic rejection, but it may also lead to dismissal from your current school, and may prevent you from going to any institution of higher learning ever again. And lying on your application is never necessary. Every person has more than enough interesting experiences to fill an application three times over. All you have to do is spend some time thinking about what is interesting about yourself.

You should also be aware that your essay is the place where you will have the chance to display all of your various traits which exhibit intangible factors the admissions committee is looking for in the candidates it sees: motivation, maturity, emotional stability, the capacity for interpersonal relations, high ideals, sound judgment, ambition, energy, leadership potential, demonstrated compassion for others, and so forth. Obviously it will not do for you simply to say, "I am mature" or "I am ambitious." But the way you present your achievements and your plans for the future, and the words you use to write about those things, can give the admissions committee an excellent view of your character. You of course need to ensure that that view is favorable and helps your admission.

Extracurricular and Community Activities: Crusader or Dilettante

If there is one issue on which all admissions officers agree, it is that they are more impressed by leadership in one or two activities than they are by membership in a hundred. Quality, not quantity, and depth, not scope, are the watchwords. Concentrate on a few things and do them well and you will be rewarded. Spread yourself too thin over many areas, and the admissions committee will consider you a joiner rather than a doer, and will be completely unimpressed.

When you present your activities to the admissions committee, remember that they are interested in detail. If you have a good number of activities or they span a long period of time, you may want to consider a resume format or a chronological list. For each activity, be sure to list which period of time you were involved—what months and years. List how many hours per week you devoted to each activity (make sure this is not an unreasonably large number, which would have left you no time to attend classes). Describe what each organization does. Assume that the reader has never heard of it, even if it is well-known or obvious from the name (your local chapter may have done something unusual). Describe in detail any leadership role you might have had. This includes both formal roles (specific offices like vice president) and informal ones (just plain organizer). If you won any awards, or were given any special commendations along the way, those should be described; in particular, you should not only name the award, but describe why it was given to you. If you were paid for your efforts, describe that. Remember what the admissions committee is interested in: details and specific instances of work accomplished.

Clearly, you should give thought to the overall picture you are trying to paint. It is almost always best to downplay activities which may represent social privilege or purely leisure activities. In addition, highlight the most dramatic activities you can find, the ones which best demonstrate your compassion for others. Do not ignore community activities; they are frequently forgotten by applicants, but can often carry more weight with an admissions committee than on-campus activities. Do not ignore religious activities you are involved in. Do not ignore anything you do as a musician, an artist, or an athlete. Any factor which adds to your personality is important to an admission committee. Remember that you do not need to present something supersophisticated in order to get a favorable response from an admissions committee. You can do very well talking about the importance of your religious beliefs to your life. If you were active in a 4–H activity, you can discuss it proudly, as it can help make you an interesting person to the most jaded urbanite. If you made a real contribution to your high school's school spirit, and you can convey that enthusiasm to the admissions committee, they may be interested in you because of your possible contribution to college activities. There is no need to report something earth-shattering; you must simply present yourself as an interesting, warm person to the committee.

The Interview: Pressure or Fun

Many colleges offer an interview to applicants, and some require it. Interviews are rare at most graduate schools; the University of Chicago Law School is the only major law school which even offers one; 20% of their applicants take advantage of the offer. And, of course, virtually all medical schools have an interview. The medical school interview will be dealt with separately below.

Except for a very occasional individual, virtually all American high school and college students speak much better than they write. Thus, unless you get particularly nervous when confronted with a somewhat pressured situation, you should leap at the chance for an admissions interview. Even if you are applying to schools where interviews are not generally offered, such as business schools, if you have something special to say you should strongly request one and see what happens; exceptions are made by admissions committees, from time to time.

The basic goal of an interview is to have a good, friendly conversation with your counterpart. A good conversation can be on any topic; it need not be related to the admissions process at all. A friend of mine once had an interview at the undergraduate division of the University of Chicago, in which a half an hour was spent discussing surfing. My friend knew absolutely nothing about surfing, but it was a good conversation. Of course, you as the applicant should be prepared to convey some substantive information to the admissions officer as well. In particular, the interview gives you the opportunity to stress the parts of your record which you think are especially strong. It also gives you the opportunity to clear up any questions or misconceptions the admissions office may have about your record or your application. (The interview should not, on the other hand, be viewed as an opportunity to give an excuse for every weakness of your record. You should stress the positive during the entire session.) Finally, the interview gives you the opportunity to tell the admissions office in person exactly how interested you are in attending the school. (You should expect to be asked to what other places you are applying.) You should make the most of your opportunity to tell them how hungry for their school you really are.

You should also expect that the admissions officer will use the interview to convey some information to you. *You must be prepared.* Inevitably the admissions officer will ask you whether you have any questions. He will gauge your real seriousness about the school by the depth of your questions. Do not, under any circumstances, ask him routine questions which can be answered by reading the catalog. Doing that can be the kiss of death for your candidacy; it shows that you have not even been interested enough to read the catalog carefully. Some types of questions to ask include: What do you think are the strengths and weaknesses of a particular department (choose one in which you have an interest)? How many faculty members does the average student know well? What speakers have come to the campus recently? What does the average student do on the weekends? What kinds of job counselling does the university provide? What kinds of employers interview on campus?

It is very rare that any bias creeps into the interview process, although it does happen occasionally. Usually the triggering factor is a deep political dispute. I only know of two instances. In one case, the candidate was the son of a man who was publicly involved in the effort to prevent busing as a means of desegregating the Boston public schools. When the son applied to Harvard College, his interviewer turned out to be a black professor, whose first question was, "Do you think it is morally defensible to oppose school desegregation in Boston?" The interview went rapidly downhill from there. On the other side of the political spectrum, Jesse Jackson, during the 1984 Presidential campaign, alleged that one of his daughters had faced racial discrimination when she was interviewed (also, ironically, for Harvard College) by an alumnus—a Chicago lawyer—who asked her pointed questions about her father's political activities. The daughter was accepted at Harvard, but chose instead to attend Howard University because of the abusive handling she had received during the interview. Such incidents are rare, but they apparently do occur. If you as a candidate are ever faced with such a situation, the best course is to report it immediately directly to the Dean of Admissions at the school involved. Every day that you wait will make your story colder, and thus less credible. You may or may not be admitted thereafter, but at least you will have done your best to report entirely inappropriate behavior to the person responsible for the entire admissions process.

As for the mechanics of an interview, you should use your common sense. Obviously, you need to be well dressed (for men, in a suit and tie, for example). You should be aware of the difference between being well dressed and dressed to the hilt; there is no need to dress as if you were about to attend a banquet at the Waldorf-Astoria. You must be punctual; being late can by itself demolish your candidacy. Finally, when you are going for your interview, your parents should not be allowed to set foot in the admissions building. You should send them off on a tour of the campus before you go for your interview, and you should meet them at some other prearranged location afterward. If the admissions officer asks where they are, tell him, "I sent them on a tour of the campus." The admissions committee has to admit you, not your parents. You should be trying to project an aura of maturity and independence, and having your parents anywhere in the vicinity is not helpful toward that goal. Nothing your parents can say to an admissions officer in person can help your chances, and there are a thousand things they can say to hurt your chances.

The Fine Art of Recommendations

Recommendations on very rare occasions help candidates. Usually they are neutral or slightly supportive; more frequently than they should, they hurt the candidate. Recommendations are supposed to be favorable; they are expected to be glowing. Thus, no matter how glowing the recommendation is, it is routine to the admissions committee. The best result of a routine recommendation is that it will support and corroborate facts you have written about in your application. If you said in an essay to a business school that you had responsibility for 50 employees, and the recommendation said you did a great job with 50 employees, then the recommendation verifies your facts and enhances your overall credibility. That is the most that can be hoped for from the average recommendation.

There are a number of different types of recommendations that can hurt you; with some, the damage is quite unintentional. The worst is a serious negative comment. No matter how deeply it is buried in a pile of positives, the serious negative will stick out like a sore thumb (this is to be compared with the negative-which-really-isn't-a-negative, such as "He tries too hard" or "He's too much of a perfectionist.") A good example appears in the DeFunis case alluded to earlier. The candidate had received a recommendation from a professor which was filled with superlatives except for one sentence. There was evidence in the case that this sentence was the principal reason why DeFunis was denied admission to the University of Washington Law School: "I admire him in his persistence, but there seems to be the slight tendency of not caring upon whom he might step in the process." No admissions committee could ignore such a candid character insight.

A second type of serious negative recommendation is one which is lukewarm, and allows the admissions committee to read between the lines that the recommender is unenthusiastic and the school could do better in selecting elsewhere from its candidate pool. Sometimes such letters are intended, sometimes not; in either case they are devastating.

A third type of negative is one which is too short; it usually results from ignorance or laziness on the part of the recommender. Two sentences of high praise is not a sufficient recommendation; the admissions committee will draw the conclusion that the recommender really doesn't know the candidate, or doesn't care about the outcome of the application. Such a letter certainly does not help you, and may well hurt you.

As a fourth category, letters from relatives are obviously not acceptable; if the relatives are alumni, perhaps an alumni telephone call might be appropriate, if to the right person at the right time. The Impassioned Family Letter is the only acceptable correspondence directly from the family to the admissions committee.

Finally, the fifth type of recommendation which can harm you is the very common VIP recommendation. "Too often candidates solicit recommendations from judges, lawyers, alumni, politicians and others solely because the writer is a public figure or has ties with the law school. Few writing these recommendations have more than a casual acquaintance with the applicant and most recommendations of this kind demonstrate the absence of a reasonable opportunity for the author to form a sound judgment of the applicant's qualifications."—Harvard Law School.

Given that recommendations can severely hurt you, the question comes to mind whether any way exists for you to screen your recommendations before they are sent to the school to which you are applying. A truly thoughtful recommender will send you or let you see a copy of the letter he has written. This happens quite often when business people are writing the recommendations, but very rarely when academics are writing. But you cannot count on being shown a copy, and it is usually quite improper to ask.

Clearly if the recommender is a very close friend, he would show you the letter and perhaps go over it with you before it is sent. A few recommenders may go so far as to allow you to prepare an outline or a first draft of the letter. This of course gives you a golden opportunity to have a recommendation zero in on exactly the areas which you believe will interest the admissions committee, and you should without doubt take the time to educate your recommender on what the committee is looking for.

Another gambit is possible if you are applying to a school which has you collect the recommendations and forward them on to the school along with your application. The recommendation is sealed in a special envelope which the recommender signs. (This system puts the full responsibility on you to make sure all items are filed; no one can hide behind the excuse that a required recommendation "got lost in the mail.") Although it is of questionable ethics, many students do the following: If they are applying, for instance, to business schools, they pick a business school which they have no interest in attending, but which has the recommendation-forwarding process just described. Perhaps the candidate decides that he will not under any circumstances go to Tuck, Dartmouth's business school, because its locale is too isolated. When the candidate goes to his recommenders, he will hand them a set of forms and envelopes including all of the business schools he is interested in plus Tuck. The recommender will write the same letter for each school, and hand them all back to the candidate. The candidate can then break the seal on the Tuck envelope and read the recommendation. If the recommendation is favorable; the candidate sends the rest off; if it is intentionally or unintentionally unfavorable, the candidate simply throws the whole bunch away and finds a new recommender who will write a good letter.

A final possibility is formal disclosure by the school to which you are applying. In the 1970's Congress passed a law, known as the Buckley Amendment, which allowed every student access to his educational files. The Buckley Amendment has two hitches, however; (1) students are allowed to waive their rights under it; and (2) you don't get to look at your file until you actually enroll at the school. Since waivers are allowed, every recommendation form contains a section where you can waive later access to the form. You should *always* agree to this waiver. If you do not waive, some of your recommenders, knowing that you will in all likelihood read the recommendation, will no longer be candid in their remarks. The danger is that they will become lukewarm, with the severe results noted above. And if you do not waive, the members of the admissions committee will no longer consider the recommendations as candid, and thus they will not be considered as seriously by the committee, no matter how favorable they may be. And you should be aware that the vast majority of applicants do waive, perhaps for the strategy reasons just noted and also out of courtesy to their recommenders, who should not have the confidential nature of their remarks compromised. The second hitch means that even if you do not waive, it will not help you be admitted to a school. You only get to see your file when you are actually enrolled in the school, months after the entire application process is completed. The Buckley Amendment can only do two things for you: it can help you expunge a false academic or disciplinary note from your permanent record; and it might give you ammunition for a lawsuit against a recommender who actually slandered you, knowingly or negligently lied about you in a recommendation to your detriment—a very rare occurrence and usually not worth suing over. The Buckley Amendment cannot help you to be accepted at the school of your choice, and you should by all means waive its meagre protections unless you have some strong moral feelings about such waivers.

The unfortunate thing about recommendations is that, even among people who do know you well and can comment authoritatively, it is probably the case that not one of them knows how to write a good recommendation. Since you do not want to leave something this important to chance, what you should do is give them some instruction on how to do it. The best recommender you can get is someone who has some special credibility with the admissions committee: Either he is a personal friend of some member of the admissions committee, or he is such a renowned scholar that they cannot ignore what he has to say. And every once in a while an individual comes along who raises the recommendation to an art form (Professor John Finley of Harvard is the classic example; he holds the record for most successful Rhodes scholarship recommendations). If such a person gives you his unqualified endorsement, you can practically write your own admission ticket. If you do not have such a person available, then virtually any teacher or employer who can follow instructions will do. Admissions committees are not particularly concerned with the identity of the writer (full professor vs. associate professor; CEO vs. Assistant Treasurer). They are interested in the content.

The writer must describe how long he has known you and in what context. He must give evidence of having had ample opportunity to see you in action. He should describe various aspects of your character, such as maturity, intelligence, drive, and ability to take responsibility, *and cite specific examples.* He should comment on why he thinks you are now ready for the study of law, or business, or whatever you are applying for. And finally, for the ideal recommendation he should make some sort of comparative assessment, either generally, "One of the three best students I have seen in 20 years," or specifically, "Better than Joe Jones, who matriculated at your school last year." This comparison is critical to put the entire analysis in perspective.

One area which perennially causes trouble for recommenders are questions which ask about the applicant's weaknesses. If the recommender gives some really serious weaknesses, then the recommendation becomes negative, and is certain to hurt the applicant. If the recommender lists no weaknesses at all, he risks being viewed as unobjective toward the candidate, and the recommendation is taken less seriously. The best approach is to list only one or two weaknesses, and they should either be mild ones, or they should be pseudo-weaknesses, as in "Cindy is too much of a perfectionist" or "Roger tries too hard." Finally, whatever the weakness might be, it is important that the reviewer say that the candidate is aware of the weakness, and is improving in the area. A comment like that can turn a seeming weakness into a real strength.

Your recommenders should not give a laundry list of your accomplishments. You should have already discussed all of those points in your portion of the application; repeating them in a recommendation will not be helpful to the committee. The decision-makers will be much more interested in specific instances where your character had a chance to be displayed to others. Finally, many form recommendations issued by schools have boxes where the recommender can check off his opinion of various aspects of your character. Such categories include Intelligence, Industry, Personality, Leadership, Personal Effectiveness, Ability to Communicate, Self-Discipline, Potential for Graduate Study, Professional Competence, Ability to Work with Others,

Achievements in Comparison with his Peers, Maturity, Initiative, Motivation, Creativeness, Managerial Potential, Clarity of Goals, and Self-Understanding. Both you and your recommender should know that only the highest two boxes should be checked, the highest percentages possible. The average recommendation is so overwhelmingly favorable in those aspects that anything less draws the scrutiny of the admissions committee.

Academic and Career Goals

Ordinarily, one's choice of major or future career choice does not play a role in the admissions process. However, there are some exceptions. If you intend to major in something exotic or undersubscribed, your chances may improve. Many Ivy League classics departments have many professors and few students; if you declare that you are planning to major in the classics, your chances for admission may improve slightly. If you are applying to law school or medical school, and you presented a credible claim that you are planning a career in legal services for the poor, or a medical career in an area of the country which needs doctors, then your chances for admission would be improved. You would have the burden of proof to show that your plan is sincere; you would probably have to show a consistent record of helping the disadvantaged.

Finally, for college admissions, there is some evidence that applicants who show some interest in a specific field have a better chance of admission than those who are completely undecided. Whether this is a cause or an effect is unclear. "The admittance rate for those who checked undecided as opposed to liberal arts or engineering was a full ten percentage points lower, than for those who had made a definite choice."—Director of Admissions, Princeton University.

Supplements to the Application

In addition to the many materials required by the formal application, many schools, especially colleges, invite you to submit virtually any additional material. You should be very wary of this invitation. There is a saying among Admissions officers, "The thicker the folder, the thicker the applicant." The weak applicant attempts through bulk to make up for a lack of quality. You should not fall into this category even by association.

Among the things you could send to colleges: paintings, drawings, tapes of musical performances, copies of a book you have written, copies of any articles you have written for major publications, poems, significant research projects, and athletic data sheets. An athletic data sheet (for an individual sport, a listing of times or other scores or achievements; for a team sport, your own scoring records as well as some information on how the team did as a whole) is an excellent idea if your record is good; if you have had something significant published, send that in as well. However, you should think very carefully about sending in anything relating to music or the arts. Every young person likes to think he is a budding talent, and most teachers in high school will not say anything to discourage you from your efforts. What you should realize is that those efforts, which are appreciated by your family and teachers, may not receive such a warm reception from a roomful of strangers. You should get candid, independent criticism before you send something artistic to an admissions committee. As for reports, term papers, projects, and the like, they are usually a wasted effort because no one has time to read them; and you always run the risk that someone on the admissions committee knows a great deal more about your subject than you do, in which case he can spot all your errors. The general rule for supplementing should be, when in doubt, don't.

Accidents of Birth

There are a few factors in the admissions picture over which you have very little control. You should take advantage of them if you can; otherwise, you should not worry, as they only help a few people enter each school each year.

Colleges, and some graduate schools, seek regional diversity among their student body. If they never even thought about the subject, they would probably get it anyway. As it is, some schools give a very small bonus for living in the right place. Harvard College favors applicants from Massachusetts; Stanford has a very high proportion of Californians. At all Ivy League and Seven Sister colleges, you have an advantage if you are from the South, the Midwest, or any rural area. (One Ivy League admissions committee has a "Boonie Day" on which all rural students are considered.) For example, for the Williams Class of 1983, New England applicants had an 18% chance of being accepted, while those from the Midwest and the South each had a 30% chance. Many state universities have the opposite bias as a result of legislative edict: Boalt Hall Law School of Berkeley takes 25% of its classes from outside California; the University of Virginia Law School takes 20% from out of state; the University of Texas at Austin Law School only takes 10%.

Alumni children—legacies—get a strong preference at most colleges, and a very weak one at most graduate schools. Yale College once announced, for example, that 20% of its classes was reserved for legacies. One fact to be alert to is that the definition of legacies varies from school to school: Some include grandchildren and nieces; others do not. A related factor to alumni ties is the background of the parents of an applicant to college. Some colleges appear to prefer candidates whose parents have gone to college, on the theory that they will be more supportive of their children's academic work (and perhaps more supportive of the new alma mater as well).

A rather controversial factor in college admissions at some colleges is the ability of the student's parents to pay tuition. There is a tier of well-endowed universities—Harvard, Yale, Wellesley, Smith, Rice—which offer admission regardless of financial need. However, there appears to be another tier of colleges which will take very able students and put them on scholarships, but will reject somewhat less able ones on the ground that the students' parents are unable to pay full or partial tuition. An article in the *New York Times Magazine* showed that much of the deliberation of the admissions committee at Vanderbilt centered on the ability of applicants' families to pay tuition. Whether this trend will expand in the future is unclear.

At the opposite end of the spectrum from schools which discriminate against students who cannot pay full tuition are those which are actively recruiting the most promising scholars. Some, like the University of Texas and Rice University, are striving to improve their reputations and the caliber of their student bodies, and are giving special attention to recruiting National Merit Scholarship Winners, for example. Other schools, however, are simply putting forward small "merit scholarships" which appeal primarily to the ego of the high school candidate; such applicants should be warned that a school which needs to dangle a bonus of a few hundred dollars cash in front of top students in order to entice them into the school should be viewed warily, and certainly those few hundred dollars are, in the long run, meaningless.

A Note to Minority Students

Although the *Bakke* case ended specific numerical quotas based on race, affirmative action is still in full swing at most colleges and universities in the United States. The list of applicants who qualify for special treatment is a long one, and varies from university to university. The following groups have been included: American Indians, Blacks, Puerto Ricans, Chicanos, Mexican-Americans, Hispanics, Philippine Americans, Oriental/Asian Americans, Appalachian whites, the handicapped, and Vietnam veterans.

The primary emphasis of members of such groups should be on showing that they are academically qualified to do the work at the particular institution they want to attend. The basic way to show such qualifications is through grades. One area in which minority students clearly get a break is that of test scores. Minorities consistently score lower on standardized tests than do others, and therefore universities often compensate for that by setting significantly lower cutoff scores, or no cutoff scores at all, for minority candidates. Once that foundation of being able to do the work has been laid, most of the other elements of the admissions picture will come together. One way to demonstrate that you are especially worthy of admission is to show how you have personally overcome discrimination and hardship. You can rest on the idea that all minorities have suffered discrimination. Or you can discuss in your application specific instances in which you personally were a victim of discrimination. In either case, you will want to explain how your fight against injustice has strengthened you, and made you a better person. On the one hand, your entire application should not revolve around the fact that you are a member of a minority group; you should not trumpet that fact to the exclusion of other aspects of your candidacy. But on the other hand, you should not obscure the fact that you are a minority either.

An interesting trend which you should watch closely is the idea that special preferences should be given to minorities only if they come from poverty or are contributing to their minority community. There exists some concern that a few applicants from affluent families are benefitting from programs designed for the disadvantaged, and that more than mere incidental membership in a minority group should be required for special treatment. A good example is Stanford Law School's application question: "If you have checked a minority category, please include statement describing in detail your ethnic, cultural and linguistic heritage, including the background of each of your parents, and note your on or off campus activities, if any, which would evidence your ethnic identity." If such questions develop into a trend, it may suggest that black students, for example, should join the black students' society at their college and perhaps the local NAACP chapter in order to build a history of activity in the community.

A Note to Older Applicants

Recently, many people in their 30's and 40's have been returning to graduate schools, both in the arts and sciences and in business and law. (Medical schools are still virtually closed to anyone over about 32, and it appears that they will remain so more or less indefinitely.)

The first thing that such older applicants should do is to cease worrying about their undergraduate grades. Any grades over five years old are suspect, and any over ten years old are barely even looked at unless they are exceptionally good or very poor. Poor undergraduate grades from long ago should not be a hindrance today if the applicant shows a real desire to learn. One way that older applicants can help themselves is to produce some excellent recent grades. This is a particularly good strategy if you have been out of school for many years and are applying to a very competitive professional school, like a major business school or law school. A large question in the admissions committee's eyes will be whether you can perform at the academic level required. If, prior to your application, you have enrolled in a Master's program and gotten all A's, you are in a much better position to argue your case. Many Master's programs are easy to get into, and fairly easy to do well in, and it may be worth your while to enroll. "Strong recent graduate work plus a strong LSAT may suggest that a weaker college record of several years ago can be largely disregarded."—University of Wisconsin Law School.

What older candidates should be concerned with is standardized tests. Whenever grades decline in importance in measuring academic potential, standardized tests fill the vacuum. Such exams are especially important in evaluating older students who have been out of school for several years, since such tests measure nimbleness of mind, which is a very important thing to have when you are returning to higher education after a considerable time away. You should be concerned especially with standardized tests because they require a mind able to jump quickly from one subject to the next. Older students usually take considerably more coaching before they understand the tricks involved in solving standardized test questions.

Finally, older students will find that a large part of their success in applying will depend on the eloquence of their essays. They must convincingly describe why they want to return to school; they must give an interesting account of what they have been doing in recent years; and they must present acceptable reasons why they should be given a graduate school seat rather than someone recently out of college. Writing the persuasive and eloquent essay is your greatest challenge, along with mastering standardized testing.

A Note to Foreign Applicants

Foreign students are very much in demand in American colleges and, to a lesser extent, in American arts and sciences graduate schools and business schools. For one thing, as a foreign student you clearly have your own niche on the diversity scale. You add a great deal to American campuses and classrooms, and thus virtually every school wants to have a good number of you.

The two strong requirements for admission to an American school for you are that you have your visa in order, and that you achieve an acceptable score on the Test of English as a Foreign Language (TOEFL). Visa requirements in every country, including the United States, are a mess, and thus you must have your papers entirely in order before schools will be interested in having you as a student. Beyond that, virtually every school has some cut-off TOEFL score, which you must surpass. Please note that the TOEFL is only really used to set a minimum and see if you can reach it. In general, American universities do not consider a very high score on the TOEFL necessary for admission to a selective school. All you need is the school's minimum, and you get no bonus for scoring above it.

Foreign students should not worry excessively about other standardized tests such as the SAT, the GMAT, or the GRE. American universities know that such standardized, multiple-choice examinations do not exist in other parts of the world. American universities know that foreign students are at a disadvantage in never having taken such tests, and admission committees generally make allowances for that handicap. What you should do is view the tests as an opportunity. If, for example, you score in the 90th percentile on a standardized test, you will have beaten not only virtually all foreign students taking it, but also 90% of native English speakers. You could then justly be proud, and most graduate schools would consider it a conspicuous accomplishment and would probably make it a very important factor in the admissions decision.

One great advantage you have, and one all foreign applicants should be aware of, is that only a handful of people in the entire United States know how to interpret your grades. It is probably true that many admissions officers here know what First Class Honors at Oxford or Cambridge represent. But if you are not from a major university in a major country of the world, interpretation becomes extremely difficult. What you should do, then, is provide with your application an explanation of your grades. An explanation could include, for example, what percent of a class receives certain types of honors, how your university is rated in your country, and how difficult your course load was. In order to be credible, such a discussion must follow the facts, but it can also show your grades in their best possible light.

Finally, a note should be made about the foreign candidate's essays. You should, of course, write the essays, and then have them edited and proofread by an American. However, the essay should not read like a perfect, completely American essay. If an admissions committee sees an absolutely perfect essay from a foreign applicant, it will assume that someone else wrote it for him, and they may reject him as a result. Ideally, the essay should contain a few minor errors in grammar and especially diction. And the errors which are made should be the types of errors made by individuals of the applicant's nationality (for example, a native German might put his English verbs at the end of his sentences). Obviously, this should not be taken too far; very bad mistakes, or too many mistakes, will clearly hurt your application. But an error-free, sanitized essay will attract too much attention and appear false: This is one situation in life where making mistakes pays.

A Note to Transfer Applicants

The basis of all transfer applications is good grades at the first school. If you want to transfer from a lower prestige school to a higher prestige one, good grades are the main criterion. If you want to transfer between schools of equal prestige, or from one of higher to one of lower, the move should be fairly automatic unless your grades are very weak. Your record prior to that achieved in your current school may be of some interest, but not a great deal.

The other aspect of transferring is that you have to give a convincing explanation of why you want to transfer. Usually, the answer that you will be closer to your boyfriend or girlfriend is not sufficient; the added prestige of the new school is not enough, since it doesn't relate personally to you, but only to the institution. And the fact that you will be closer to home at the new school, or the fact that you are generally unhappy where you are now, is not enough.

There is only one tried-and-true method to present a successful transfer application. First, you must say that you have an academic desire to study a certain subject, perhaps a sub-specialty in a field. Then you have to say that your current school does not meet your specific academic needs (at this stage you can couple your argument with the thought that your current school does not provide sufficient challenges for you.) Finally, as the last piece in the puzzle, you "discover" that the school you want to attend has exactly the program you want. If all of this is presented reasonably and credibly, and you have good grades, you should have no problem. One thing you should keep in mind as you present your case for a transfer: You should try to avoid at any time denigrating or complaining about the old school you want to leave. The new school does not have an interest in having someone in its student body who is quick to find fault in everything, never satisfied or happy. You should merely seem disappointed in your old school, never bitter.

CHAPTER 3
Planning an Effective Strategy: A Step-by-Step Approach

So your grades didn't set the world on fire. Maybe you had a B average, maybe a C+. So you didn't score in the top 10% of the SATs, the LSATs, or the GMATs. Maybe you've never done well on standardized tests; maybe you had a bad day; maybe five of the eight sections on your GMAT were math, and you hate math; maybe you just hate standardized tests. So you weren't Big Man (or Woman) on Campus in extracurricular activities. Maybe you signed up for a few clubs; maybe you just spent most of your spare time with your friends, rather than with organized groups.

So what do you do now?

First of all, you have to realize that inevitably you will be grouped in the Average/Borderline category at competitive schools to which you are applying. Secondly, you should realize that you have lots of company. The majority of applicants to the schools you want to go to, and probably the majority of applicants who are accepted at those schools, fall into your category. Thus, your objective should be to differentiate yourself from the other members of the vast Average/Borderline group. Finally, you should realize that a key factor in the decisions made about you will be what you say in your application. So a great deal of your success or failure still rests in your hands.

If you find yourself in the Average/Borderline category at the schools which you most want to attend, there are two things you must do as a matter of self-defense. You must apply to some "safety" schools, some less-competitive schools where you will be either a Definite Admit or very high in their Average/Borderline group. Even if at the beginning of the admissions season you think that it is beneath your dignity to apply to safety schools, you should grit your teeth and do so anyway. There is absolutely no more disheartening feeling in the world than being rejected everywhere you apply; even an acceptance from a lesser-known school will feel good in the long run. Perhaps you have an inflated picture of your chances of admission (perhaps your advisors have told you that you are a shoo-in at Princeton, without any objective basis to back it up); better to have one or two safeties in your pocket if the opinions of the schools to which you are applying happens to differ from yours. And perhaps you have overlooked the merits of schools which are small, or are in a different region of the country from your home, or have less well-developed reputations; by choosing one of these as a safety you may be enhancing your chances of getting a good education. And finally, if you have no safeties and are rejected everywhere, your choices will be *extremely* limited. In June, three months before the new term starts, virtually all schools will be filled to capacity. Your choice may boil down to waiting an entire year before applying again, or applying to very mediocre schools which might be willing to open a place for you. Either option will probably be hard to accept and certainly less palatable than going to one of the safety schools which would have happily admitted you in October.

The second self-defense measure you must take, if you are an Average/Borderline candidate, is to apply to lots of schools, as many as you think are worthwhile. If you insist on applying to very competitive schools, you should at least cover yourself by applying to a good number of them. Your chances of admission might be 10% at each. But you really have no idea which of the schools will decide you have the qualities they want. Of course, you dramatically increase your chances of getting into at least one by putting your eggs into many baskets.

The advice I have just tendered goes against what many guidance counsellors and admissions officers will tell you. Often they are great advocates of the idea that less is better, and that you should only apply to five schools, for example. (Exeter goes so far as to prohibit its students from applying to more than a specified number of Ivy League colleges.) Why do they give this advice? Because they are concerned about reducing the caseload of admissions applicants. Every extra application means more work for the guidance counsellor in terms of writing a recommendation and counselling the applicant. Every extra application means more work for admissions officers who must review and debate each application. So it is in their interest to keep the total number of applications down. But that does not mean that it is in *your* interest to limit the number of your applications.

Clearly, sending out many applications has its costs. You must pay whatever fee is required. You must spend time—often a great deal of time—filling out the application. You must spend time rounding up recommendations and transcripts. So you should not go overboard. You should not apply to schools at which you clearly have no reasonable chance. Yale Law School, for instance, issues a grid which shows the number of applicants and the number accepted for various combinations of LSAT scores and undergraduate GPA's. If your combination had 0 admitted out of 230 applicants last year, you can safely skip applying to Yale.

At the other extreme, if you know that you will be accepted at Emory (your grades are well above the average of those they accept; members of the class ahead of you at your high school with weaker records had no trouble being accepted; the Emory admissions office has told you that they see no problem), and you would rather go to Emory than the University of Georgia, then there is no reason to add the University of Georgia as an additional safety school. You want to make many applications when you are an Average/Borderline candidate at many roughly comparable schools. Then you should apply to all which you would seriously consider going to, on the theory that the more you apply to, the better are your chances of being accepted to at least one.

Now to consider some specific ingredients in the strategy for the Average/Borderline candidate:

Grades: If your grades are average, or just fair, the basic objective should be to keep the admissions officer's attention focused in other directions. Your grades will usually speak for themselves; what you should be doing is highlighting other portions of your record so your grades become less important.

Keeping in mind that you want to divert the admissions officer's attention away from your grades, it is usually a mistake to make alibis in your application for your weak grades. This should be avoided unless absolutely necessary. Nothing is more effective in causing an admissions officer to focus on your grades than your offering an excuse for them. If you offer an alibi, the admissions officer is then honor-bound to check it out; he must carefully examine each item on your transcript, at the very least, and will perhaps even go so far as to call your guidance counsellor or someone familiar with your school in order to get further information. This is clearly the last thing you want, since any weakness in your record will inevitably be illuminated.

In addition, unless you have a very good alibi, the admissions officer will probably remain unmoved. Almost anyone who has gone to high school or college has faced some sort of hardship: emotional setbacks, deaths in the family, the need for a part-time job. Given that most people have gone through something of this kind, colleges and graduate schools are interested in candidates who were strong enough to overcome the hardship, and were able to get good grades in spite of it. Thus, demonstrating hardship and then admitting that you failed to overcome it is unlikely to get you very far.

There are two occasions where alibis may help you. One is when the hardship is so great that no reasonable person would expect you to overcome it. For example, if you immigrated to the United States from Taiwan at age 18 and did poorly in college English classes, that would be understandable. You should simply make a note somewhere in your application to the effect that, "Although I did well in science and math classes, I had some trouble in required English classes because I had no previous training in writing analytical essays about English literature." The other instance in which an alibi is permissible is when you have a bad grade which is a temporary aberration. If you were severely sick during a particular semester, and it is visible that your grades suffered that semester, then you should mention that cause. If you took a math or science course that was much too difficult for your background and aptitude, and you did poorly, then the circumstances can be mentioned. But even in such instances, it is best to keep the excuse as short and to the point as possible.

If you took a particularly difficult course of study in comparison with other students from your school, it would be worth mentioning. As was noted earlier where grades are discussed in more depth, you should not expect that the admissions committee will be aware of the difficulty of your course load simply by looking at your transcript. You will need to highlight the fact in your application. However, as an alibi, a discussion of how difficult your courses were is unlikely to excuse a weak record. The question immediately comes to mind, if the courses were too difficult for you, why didn't you take a more sensible load? Better to do well in a moderately difficult curriculum than poorly in an extremely difficult one.

Finally, you should be conscious of the fact that no alibi is worth anything if it is based on something over which you had control. For example, the excuse that you did poorly in school because your bad friends influenced you and led you astray, or because you were too busy attending dorm parties, is not going to get you anywhere. If your personal choices led to a disappointing GPA, you should stifle the impulse to be candid and simply let your grades speak for themselves.

Test Scores: As you are reading this book, your test scores may still be under your control if you have not already taken the relevant exam. If you think you may find yourself in the Average/Borderline category, it is clearly in your best interests to learn through a preparation course or book of some kind. Given that you are going to be in the Average/Borderline category along with hundreds if not thousands of other students, it is important for you to find an area where you can distinguish yourself from the mass. Perhaps test scores will be the vehicle. Many schools, especially schools which are actively attempting to improve their prestige and status, will attempt to increase the average test scores of their entering class. In order to do that, they will have to admit many students with high scores, and thus they may well be inclined to accept students who have good scores but are weak in other areas.

Also, you should be aware that the Average/Borderline category is usually so large that trivial differences between candidates often distinguish between acceptance and rejection. A test score just a few points higher than another candidate with otherwise similar credentials may cause your candidacy to triumph in head-to-head competition. A good solid score may lift you above the average, while nothing will so indelibly stamp your file as average than a mediocre test score.

One practical note: You should do all of your studying and take whatever courses you are going to take before you take the exam the first time. A common mistake students make is to take the exam in question the first time without any real study, do poorly, and then run out and take a course. Doing this is of some value, since your score will probably increase the second time. But since virtually all schools to which you will apply will average your two scores, whatever improvement you show will be cut in half. It is much, much smarter to get whatever improvement you can during the period before you take the exam the first time. You will be at peak performance when you take the exam the first time, and probably you will not have to repeat the exam either.

As with grades, it is usually a mistake to alibi for mediocre test scores. Your objective should be to distract the admissions officer's attention away from your scores, not to call further attention to them. The only two instances in which a standardized test alibi is at all useful is if you have a documented history of doing poorly on such tests while getting good grades, or if you were seriously ill on the day of the exam. Otherwise, you should let them stand alone, or at the very most take the exam a second or third time if you think you can achieve a significant improvement.

Work Experience: Here lies a real opportunity for the Average/Borderline candidate. First, you should catalog everything you ever did for a buck. Were you a sales clerk in a store? A waiter or waitress? A short-order cook? Did you mow lawns for your neighbors? Do gardening for Aunt Sally? Participate in experiments for the psychology department? Work as a typist or secretary? Tutor other students? Scan your experiences for anything job-related, no matter how short-term or seemingly dull.

Next, you should catalog all of the things you did as a volunteer. Were you ever an intern? Did you ever work for a public official or a political candidate? Did you ever work as a candy striper in a hospital? Did you ever address envelopes for a charitable organization or an arts group? Did you ever do some free research for a teacher or professor?

Once you have cataloged your activities, you are in a position to use them in your application. The important thing is not the content of the jobs which you have had, but rather their packaging. Except for something truly extraordinary, the prestige rating of your job is of absolutely no importance. Admissions officers have seen it all, and are not going to be especially impressed with most jobs you are able to come up with. (There are some exceptions. If you actually published a book; if you were the chief campaign manager for a significant political candidate; if you built up a business of your own.) And on the other hand, admissions officers are not going to hold against you the fact that you held lowly, menial jobs.

How do you package your job experience? Packaging comes in three parts. First is a vivid description of your actual job function. Notice the important word *vivid*. You can have the greatest job in the world, but if you describe it poorly it will not help you. Likewise, you can have a very boring, mundane job, but if you describe it well, it can be of great benefit to you. The key to vividness is detail. Generalities are rarely interesting; specifics allow the reader to experience your own experiences vicariously, which makes the writing much more interesting. Write out a description of what you did at the various jobs which you have held, one job at a time. Then, starting from your bare-bones description, use vivid adjectives and adverbs to beef up the discussion. Then, pick one or two of your jobs where something interesting happened while you were working—some incident. Describe the incident; then make the incident more interesting to the reader by using better, more exciting words. Don't be afraid to make the description personal. Describe how you solved a problem, how you turned a doubting potential customer into a buyer, how your boss was about to fire you but you convinced him that you were really doing your job properly, and so on. Once you have completed the essay on your job experiences, give it to *several* thoughtful people to read. Ask them specifically to make suggestions for changes. Most of your reviewers should say, "I liked this section, expand it with more details. I thought this other section moved slowly, shorten it a bit." Once you combine these criticisms into a workable essay, and once you have made sure the essay flows nicely, that it has mistakes in neither grammar nor spelling, you will have a good addition to any application.

The second part of your packaging, which should be briefer than your job description, should address the question of what you learned from your job. Even if you held the most unexciting job in the United States, it is possible for you to have learned a great deal from it.

- **You could have learned what qualities are needed to be a good subordinate.**

- You could have learned, by observing your boss, what qualities are needed to be a good boss.
- You could have learned what methods can be used to motivate employees.
- You could have learned how to manipulate a bureaucracy to get something done.
- You could have gained insight into how people make decisions.
- You could have gained insight into human nature by watching how people act under pressure.

The things which can be learned from a job situation are almost endless in variety. You should choose a few of the things you have learned, describe them, and highlight them with examples. Again, you should be concrete and specific, in order to hold the reader's interest; platitudes will simply not do.

The third and final part of your packaging, which should be even briefer than the description of what you learned from your job, should be a description of why what you have learned is relevant to the education you now want to undertake. One possibility is that your job experience is indirectly relevant. It demonstrates that you have a strong desire to learn, since you were willing to undertake part-time work in order to help pay for your education (or save for the future). And your job experience makes you a more thoughtful, interesting person when compared with someone who has never worked.

The other possibility is that your job experience is directly relevant to the education you want to undertake. For business school, any work experience is automatically directly relevant. For law school, legal experience can be used as evidence of your strong motivation to study law; medical work experience does the same for medical school. If you have had work experience applicable to a possible major (such as work in a science lab, work on a school newspaper, or tutoring of students), then that work can be cited as directly relevant to your desire to go to college or graduate school. In either event, remember that you must be specific in any of your comments; vague platitudes are likely to hurt you, not help you.

Your strategy with respect to work experience should seem fairly simple, and it is: Describe what you did, what you learned from it, and why it will make you a better student and a more interesting person. And when writing your essay, you should always be specific rather than general. If this advice is so simple, is it really effective? The answer is absolutely yes. The reason is that only an extremely small number of applicants succeed in packaging their work experience correctly. The norm is no mention of work experience at all, or only a very brief list, or at best a short description filled with generalities and platitudes. By following the formula just given, you will set yourself apart from 99.9% of the applicants who are seeking admission to the schools to which you are applying. Work experience alone will not guarantee you admission somewhere, but the goal is to elevate yourself from the great mass of Average/Borderline candidates. A good, concise, clear exposition of your work experience can do the trick, and significantly improve your chances for admission at competitive schools.

Extracurricular and Community Activities: Everything which has just been said about work experience is directly applicable to extracurricular and community activities. You should approach them in a basically identical way.

The first step is to catalog everything you have ever done, even as the lowliest participant.

- **Are you a member of any clubs?**
- **Do you play any sports, even just for personal pleasure outside of organized teams?**
- **Do you play any musical instruments?**
- **Have you done any writing for a newspaper, or even just for yourself?**
- **Have you worked on any science experiments outside of required class exercises?**
- **Do you have any hobbies?**
- **Do you follow politics?**
- **Have you ever done anything artistic?**
- **Have you ever done anything to help other people, either by yourself or in an organized way?**
- **Have you ever helped a charity or other nonprofit group?**
- **Have you ever done anything involving your church or synagogue?**
- **Have you ever done anything to improve life in your community?**

An important thing to remember about extracurricular and community activities is that it is never too late to start (so long as you start before you file your application). It is probably true that, all else being equal, an admissions committee will prefer to see a history of three years of involvement in an activity rather than three months. But an activity of three months described thoroughly is more valuable to a candidate than three years of involvement poorly or weakly described. Again, packaging is critical.

Once you have prepared your catalog, you will be ready to use it in your application. The basic rule of extracurricular activities is that what counts is quality, not quantity. At some point in the application, you may be asked to list your extracurricular and community activities. There you should put your catalog. Elsewhere in your application, however, you may be asked to describe those activities, or talk about those which have been most important to you. It is a fatal mistake, with a question like that, to respond with the catalog. The admissions committee is not asking for a list of all the clubs you were able to join. If the application seeks a descriptive answer, you must provide a descriptive answer. And in order to give such an answer, you must be selective: You must choose from among your various activities and pick out one or two, or at most three, which are the most interesting. Pick the ones which have been most important to you, which are the most intrinsically interesting, or about which you can provide the most vivid descriptions.

Once you have chosen the extracurricular activities to highlight, you should use the same approach suggested for work experience:

- **You should describe them in the most interesting way possible, using concrete examples.**
- **You should explain what you learned from them, and how they changed you as a person.**
- **You should explain how they are pertinent to your further education.**

You should keep in mind throughout that you are a storyteller, about yourself, and a story is always better if it holds the reader's interest. It is very easy to write glowing generalities; such writing is also extremely boring to read, and thus will not help your application. You must always aim to be concrete and interesting.

Accidents of Birth: There are a number of factors in the admissions process over which you have no control. Every school seeks some modicum of diversity: students of different races, from different parts of the country, from urban backgrounds and from rural backgrounds, alumni children, and so on. If you fall into a category which the school to which you are applying might find interesting or desirable, you need to remember to highlight the fact in your application. Remember that the school may not be aware, or may not remember, that you are a member of a group which gets bonus points in the admissions process. You should bring it up in the application as your insurance against a forgetful admissions committee.

The flip side is that you should not dwell for any period of time on the subject. If a major portion of your application revolves around the fact that the school would have a more diverse class if they chose you because you are from rural Georgia, because you are a Seventh-Day Adventist, because you plan to major in astronomy, or because your father is a loyal alum, your entire application will be viewed with suspicion. The admissions committee will wonder whether there is really an individual behind the application, or only a convenient set of labels. All you should do is mention the special attribute in passing, and perhaps weave it into other portions of your essays, but not go further.

The one exception to this rule is that if you are a member of a racial minority group, it is not only acceptable, it is often a good idea to discuss in some depth what it is like to be a member of your minority in America, and how the fact that you are a minority has shaped your outlook on life and on the world around you. Again, it is critically important to be concrete and specific; vague generalities about American society in the twentieth century are not enough.

Your Application: In addition to the specific topics mentioned above, you will probably be asked in your applications to write a Personal Statement, an essay on any topic which interests you. If you do not have the opportunity elsewhere in the application to talk about your extracurricular and community activities and your job experiences, you may want to consider building your Personal Statement around those discussions. If you do have the opportunity elsewhere in the application to make those points, it is a major mistake to rehash what you have said about those topics in writing your Personal Statement. The topic for your Personal Statement should be something not developed elsewhere.

Your first step in preparing a Personal Statement should be to choose a topic. Choosing a topic is probably half the battle. Note the crucial word "Personal." Your essay must in some significant way relate to you personally. You may have interesting and valid things to say about the Cuban Missile Crisis, but it is difficult for you to build a case that it affected your own life in a personal way. That makes it a poor topic for your Personal Statement.

The second half of the Personal Statement battle, as with other essays on the application, is to make your essay interesting. In order to be interesting you must be specific. And you must let friends, counsellors, and teachers read your essay so you can expand the interesting portions and edit the dull ones. A separate chapter of this book is devoted to the Personal Statement, and you should read that chapter for further suggestions.

The application and Personal Statement can help the Average/Borderline candidate in another way as well. The application of the typical candidate tends to be a mess. Pages are dog-eared; coffee stains are visible; often portions are handwritten instead of typed; spelling and punctuation are sometimes wrong; when the application is typed, it is often full of corrections and otherwise sloppy. The unprofessional application is the norm at virtually every school (even at business schools, where it is quite a serious handicap for the applicant). It is my opinion that a letter-perfect application will serve to distinguish an Average/Borderline candidate from the others in that category. For one thing, to turn in a perfect application shows great respect for the school to which you are applying, which may well be reciprocated by the school. For another thing, your application will show you to be conscientious, thorough, mature, and professional. And finally, since so few applicants do turn in perfect or close to perfect applications, you will stand out just by being different. The only caveat to this strategy is that you do not want to appear to have a sanitized application which has been, in reality, prepared by your parents. Therefore, you should not seek out the most expensive word processing equipment; you should simply do the most professional job possible on an ordinary typewriter.

Recommendations: A good deal of discussion has been offered earlier in this book on recommendations, so only a few notes will be given here.

There are really only three hard-and-fast rules on who your recommenders should be:

1. Obviously, they cannot be related to you, nor can they be friends your own age;

2. Your recommenders must be people who know you well. A recommendation from an obscure assistant professor who can speak convincingly about you because he really knows you is almost always better than one from a famous scholar who has met you twice and whose letter shows that he is not really in a position to evaluate you;

3. Your recommenders must be able to write well and have some understanding of what the admissions committee wants. Your recommender can be in a perfect position to evaluate you, and can be the most enthusiastic person in the world, but if he writes poorly or fails to tell the committee what it is interested in knowing, the recommendation will be counterproductive.

Usually teachers make the best recommenders. They have written lots of recommendations before, so at least they are in practice, and they are usually fairly good writers. Employers can be good recommenders because they are often extremely enthusiastic and willing to give superlative reviews if you have done a good job for them. Unfortunately, they rarely know what it is admissions committees are looking for. What you will need to do is to read the sections of this book that deal with recommendations, and then educate your recommender before he or she writes the piece.

Other possible recommenders include coaches, clergymen, supervisors in extracurricular or community activities, and other people you have had significant contacts with in an academic or professional setting. Like employers, they will usually need some advice on what admissions committees are interested in.

Finally, friends of the family are usually a bad idea. Inevitably, their bias comes oozing out, or they demonstrate that they don't know you very well, or they demonstrate that they know you well socially, but don't have the slightest knowledge about your intellectual capacities. Other times they have little idea about what the admissions committee is looking for, or they write poorly. And even if they do turn in a good performance, the admissions committee will discount it. The committee will wonder why you had a family friend write. Was it that you didn't have any teachers who knew you well enough? Family friends should be avoided except as a last resort.

Recommendations will rarely make or break the Average/Borderline candidate, unless they are negative, in which case they will probably destroy the candidacy. Assuming that you can secure favorable recommendations, it is still important that you get the best available. In the Average/Borderline group, admissions decisions are often made after head-to-head competition of one candidate against another. Every portion of the application helps, and other things being equal, recommendations can be the decisive factor.

CHAPTER 4
The Personal Statement: Getting Your Message Across on Paper

Virtually every college and graduate school at some point in its application gives you a chance to say anything you would like to say. This section of the application is known as the personal statement.

Some schools give you a specific word limit. Fordham Law School allows you 250 words; the University of Virginia Law School allows you 200; Brooklyn Law School allows you 150. When you are given specific word limits you must be sure that you do not exceed them. For all you know, those schools have each hired a clerk who actually counts the words in each essay, automatically rejecting all applicants whose essays go over the limit. Schools that use such a limit say that the purpose is to see whether you can express yourself in a concise way, and to see whether you can follow an arbitrary rule set for you. The real reason is that the members of the admissions committee do not want to spend their time doing a lot of reading, so they place a ridiculously small limit on you. Personally, I think it is insulting for a school to do this, as if you have nothing worthwhile to say, but since it is their rule you must follow it if you wish to apply.

A very similar personal statement is one with a page limit, or one which requires an answer "in the space below." In such instances, the important thing is that you not write so small that no one can read your work, and that you not write so much that you end up being squeezed into the corner of the page. Not only must the personal statement be typed and well written, it also must be pleasing to the eye on the page.

Finally, some schools allow you as much space as you want to use. The crucial thing there is to avoid writing an opus on everything that has happened in your life and Western civilization. Two or three double-spaced typed pages is the maximum length with which you will be certain to hold the reader's attention. By all means, keep the personal statement brief.

Zen and the Art of Writing an Application

The personal statement is the only time, other than during an interview, when you can present your full personality to the admissions committee. They will have all the grades and test scores and all of the other quantitative information in front of them. The personal statement will be one of the only times you will be presented to the admissions committee in other than numerical form. On all other occasions, the educational establishment will have reduced you to a figure, something inhuman and easily understood. But there is no real way to reduce a personal statement to numbers; it must simply be read. So you should make the most of your opportunity.

The personal statement is designed to be a rather serious piece of introspection. The admissions committee wants to see how self-aware you are. In addition, it cares about the content of your statement, the facts you are conveying, and your writing style. Thus, the personal statement presents a triple task.

The personal statement should be about yourself. And that poses a problem. Most people are used to thinking about themselves all the time. But writing about oneself is very rarely done in our society. From time to time one prepares a resume, but that is a very cold, formalized style of writing, and thus much more manageable. One may write about oneself to friends in terms of activities or plans, as in, "I am going to Boston this weekend." But those comments about oneself concern the commonplace, not one's life plan.

The personal statement, then, is one of the few times in a person's life that he must take stock of where he stands and what the future holds. That can be a very unfamiliar experience for some people, and a very wrenching one for others. And to compound the problem, this written assessment of one's life is to be quasi-public; an admissions committee will read it and ponder it. This is not the most comfortable of situations for a person to be in.

Consequently, the first thing you need to do for the exercise is to put yourself in the right frame of mind to write a good piece. You should realize that the admissions committee is completely anonymous to you. You have never met any of its members; you don't even know who they are, except for the Dean of Admissions. If you don't go to the school to which you are writing, you will never see any of the people. If you do go there, the Dean of Admissions is likely to have such a low profile that you will never meet him. And even if you were to meet the dean and the entire admissions committee, they have each seen 50,000 personal statements before yours and 5,000 after, and none of them would have the slightest recollection of your essay, let alone be able to connect you with your essay. Sending a personal statement to an admissions committee is like telling a secret to an amnesiac: You are as safe as the day before.

Next you need to convince yourself of the need to write a good personal statement. Unless you are a Definite Admit, you are going to need to muster all the admissions aid you can get. Every year a few students get into the schools of their choice based on the personal statement alone. And many others are aided, or hurt, by the personal statement they write.

Writing a good personal statement entails writing about yourself. Thus, in order for your application to succeed, you must write candidly about your life. If one is going to write about oneself, what aspect of one's character does one choose? Perhaps the University of Chicago Law School application can provide some guidance: "It may be helpful to know that essays which have a narrow focus are generally more interesting to read than those which try to make a broad integration of the law with one's career or scholarly goals." You should focus on an aspect of yourself which would prove interesting to your readers. One starting point is to consider that you can either talk about something not mentioned elsewhere, or you can magnify something mentioned briefly somewhere else in the application.

Absolutely the best topic you can discuss is how you overcame adversity. If possible, talk about how you overcame hardship in your personal life (different from your academic or extracurricular biography). The hardship involved could have been poverty, racial discrimination, having one or no parents, physical handicaps, educational disadvantage (being forced to go to lousy schools, living in a rural or inner-city area where there is little emphasis on education), a language handicap (quite common among immigrants), or a combination of these factors. Then you should go on to describe how you overcame the hardships placed in your way: You got a decent education while working to support yourself and perhaps your family; you got an education despite a poor school and no encouragement, or despite physical handicaps, language problems, or racial discrimination.

If you feel you have not faced hardship in life, then another good personal statement topic is a description of a major, difficult project which you were instrumental in taking from start to finish. Explain why the project was difficult. Use a journalistic narrative to describe the project and its history. Discuss what you learned by doing it: the importance of organization and follow-through; the difficulty of teamwork; unexpected obstacles which appeared;

the difficulty of convincing politicians or bureaucrats to focus on your problem and help solve it, etc. Finally, describe how the effort helped you gain insight into your own strengths and weaknesses (the project will not have been really worthwhile unless you also learned something about yourself).

If you have no such major project, then another possibility is to discuss a single incident which helped you learn something about yourself. For example, a book you read which changed your thinking (be careful not to chose something trite like Kahlil Gibran or Jonathan Livingston Seagull); a family event, such as the death of a family member, or a serious family argument; any incident which taught you about the character of other people or about yourself. Describe someone you have met or read about who inspired you, including the specific qualities which drew you to the person, and the actual influence he or she has had on your life.

It also does not hurt to give your application a slightly foreign twist. American students who can demonstrate substantial exposure to a foreign culture often have a diversity aspect to add to a class. If you have lived in a foreign country as a child, or lived in a foreign country as an exchange student, or spent your Junior Year abroad, or simply have travelled widely, those facts should be mentioned, and you should comment on how your experiences cause you to see the world in a different way. One caveat: many Junior Year abroad programs are widely known to be soft academically. Thus if you went on one, whether it was soft or not, it is important that you spend a little time in your application talking about its difficult academic aspects.

Topics to Avoid Like the Plague

The personal statement gives you the widest possible range of topics, but there are certain ones you should avoid at all costs.

Do not write on an international, national, or local topic of interest. The admissions committee is interested in you, not in any specific opinions you might have. It is very doubtful that you will come up with any new ideas on, say, the Mideast conflict. If you do come up with a new idea, it will probably have a hole in it large enough to drive a Sherman tank through. And you run a serious danger of seeming trite, unimaginative, and impractical. For example, "The way to start solving the Mideast problem is to have everyone, Jews, Moslems, and Christians sit down at one table and talk about what they have in common." Any such little sermonette is bound to bore the admissions officer.

Do not give a capsule summary of your record. This will bore the admissions officer as well; he is able to evaluate your record entirely on his own.

And by simply offering a warmed-over rehash in your personal statement, you seem unimaginative, with nothing better to say.

Do not tell the admission's officer what his or her job is, or what he or she should look for in a candidate.

Do not talk about what college is all about, or what the law is, or what makes a good manager ("the community of learning and scholarship...").

Do not use the personal statement to give excuses for past failures, ("I would have done better if...").

Finally, avoid cliches ("athletics teaches a person the value of team-work..."), do not quote rock stars (save that for high school), and try to avoid writing an essay on finding yourself ("Let me be me.").

Do not write an essay which is too slick. It is true that part of your purpose in writing an application is to sell yourself to the admissions committee. But this must never be done in an overt, "Madison Avenue" style. Too much polish will be regarded very negatively. (Some applicants have gone so far as to take the final step and submit professionally printed brochures about themselves as part of their college applications. That will insure a quick rejection at most schools.) The committee will be making an effort to discover what you are really like, and if they think you are purposely attempting to put over a sanitized, false front, they will quickly lose enthusiasm for your application. If your parents (or you) have experience in marketing or advertising, use that experience sparingly, lest you accidentally make yourself appear too smooth for the admissions committee's taste.

Do not write a gimmick essay, unless you have little chance at a school and think it might enable you to "sneak in." There are stories which circulate the admissions world about gimmick applications that worked: the poem written as the personal statement; an account of the author's first love affair as the personal statement; a recipe for a Russian dish which got an amateur gourmet cook an admission into Harvard Law School (the members of the admissions committee reportedly actually prepared the dish and really liked it). Sometimes the gimmick is a particular stylistic device, such as "Presenting My Case to the Jury" for a law school application. It is true that from time to time a person who submits such a personal statement will be admitted to a big name school. But the simple fact is the number of times the cute, gimmick strategy is successful is far outweighed by the number of times it has failed. The usual response will be for the admissions committee to get a good laugh, and then quickly reject the candidate. In the occasional instances where the gimmick approach has worked, the candidate was usually a star Definite Admit anyway, and the application showed that there was a lighter side to his outstanding academic work. And even in those cases, the applicant probably put himself in unnecessary jeopardy. The only time a gimmick approach is warranted in when the applicant has basically no hope of being accepted on academic credentials, but the possibility exists that the committee will be so charmed that they will admit him anyway. (The most imaginative example I have seen was a student at an all-male prep school who went to his Harvard College interview dressed completely in drag. He was not accepted.) But even as a last resort, the gimmick approach is never recommended.

Write a serious essay, not a juvenile one; write on a topic that touches your own heart in a genuine way, don't simply string together a set of platitudes. Make sure the personal statement gives the admissions committee a positive picture of you.

How to Write Effectively and Clearly

Good writing is, of course, an art form. But it can be learned, and there are fundamentally good and bad techniques which you should know about. To write a personal statement, a very short essay, you must be organized. After you have chosen your topic, make a short list of the ideas you want to cover in the passage. Once you have the ideas written down, organize them into an outline, so you know what comes first and what second. Then write a first draft of the essay.

All writing consists of paragraphs, sentences, and words. Make sure that your personal statement is broken up into paragraphs; nothing looks worse than a personal statement which is just one huge paragraph. As for sentences, the key is to vary their structures and their lengths. Don't have all your sentences march from noun to verb to object. Use opening clauses; use compound sentences, complex sentences, and compound-complex sentences. And although you may admire Hemingway, don't write like him; nothing but short, choppy sentences soon wears on the reader.

As for individual words, use the vocabulary of an intelligent person your age or slightly older. Do not go overboard in using $5 words where 25¢ words will do. You need not be William F. Buckley. And under no circumstances ever use a giant word surrounded by puny words in the middle of a sentence. Such a beached whale can only be displeasing to the reader's eye.

As for style, use your own as it has developed. Write in a direct manner, as if you were having a conversation, while leaving out the most colloquial and conversational words. At all costs avoid being verbose or pompous; nothing will make the admissions committee cringe more quickly. Also, make sure you have smooth transitions from one idea to the next, from one paragraph to the next. Avoid having a choppy connection, or no connection at all. Finally, put together a temporary brain trust to edit your writing and proofread it. You may need to go through several versions of the personal statement before it begins to feel smooth. And, of course, you need to proofread the essay twice (preferrably by two different people).

As for mechanics, if you are applying to graduate schools, your goal should be to look professional; use the best typewriter you can get, preferrably an IBM Selectric. If you are applying to college, your goal should be simply to look mature. Therefore, you should very definitely type the personal statement, but use a simple typewriter. Do not have your father's or mother's secretary type an absolutely perfect piece on an office typewriter. That will be a sanitized essay, and the admissions committee will wonder if your parents *wrote* the essay as well. Do the job as carefully as possible, on a simple machine, yourself.

CHAPTER 5
Special Admissions Concerns

College

The basic manifesto of the college admissions system for competitive, private colleges, appeared in the March, 1978 issue of Harper's Magazine. The article, entitled "The College Admissions Game," was written by Richard Moll, an admissions officer at the University of California, and formerly one at Vassar, Harvard, and Yale. Moll identified five distinct categories of admissions candidates:

1. "The Intellects": students who show great academic promise, and are admitted regardless of their other qualities (this group constitutes about 10-15% of each entering class at Harvard College, so you can imagine how small it is at most colleges. What this means is that if you can portray yourself as being in this category, being accepted at top colleges will be quite easy).
2. "The Special Talent Category": basically top varsity athletes, but also an occasional musician or actor, admitted as long as the admission committee believes they can survive academically (members of this group are generally expected to be stars, not just varsity material).
3. "The Family Category": legacies, and especially legacies whose families and alumni allies put on some sort of a campaign for the candidate's admission.
4. "The Social Conscience Category": affirmative action candidates.
5. "The All-American Kid Category": the vast majority of applicants, and probably a majority of the freshman class as well, everyone not in 1–4 above.

Easily the most successful applicants are those who not only fall into categories 1–4, but who also manage to combine two categories. A minority-athlete, and a legacy-athlete, are common combinations.

For the candidate who finds himself in the "All-American Kid Category," the strategy should be the same as for every other member of an Average/ Borderline category. He must try to differentiate himself from the rest of the pack, in particular by writing an interesting essay.

Most colleges appear to rank their applicants on two scales, an academic scale and a nonacademic scale. The two are usually evenly weighted; a candidate who is extraordinary in either will probably be admitted. Such a system also helps the "All-American Kid" to some extent, since if he can rank high enough on the academic scale, there are usually lots of nonacademic factors which will provide a high overall score and thus secure admission. In contrast, a student with a very weak academic score is unlikely to be admitted with less than the most outstanding extracurricular credentials.

There appears to be some evidence that the percentage of students accepted through the "Special Talent" category tends to get larger as the school itself gets smaller. The theory goes as follows: no orchestra can go forward without a tuba player; at a large school, there are bound to be several tuba players in each class simply by the law of averages, and at least one will probably be drawn to the orchestra; in a small school, however, a tuba player might only come along once every four or five years; but the orchestra must have a tuba player, so, therefore, average tuba playing ability can become a "Special Talent" in some years, and the percentage of "Special Talent" admissions rises. As a practical matter, what this means for a high school student is that if you have some slightly unusual interests or abilities, it may pay for you to scatter a good number of applications (stressing those interests and abilities) to competitive, smaller colleges, in the hope that one of them will happen to need your particular skills.

You should also be aware that many Ivy League schools have what is called the "Happy Bottom Quarter." The theory is that if Princeton, for instance, took only straight A students from high school (which they could easily do, given their huge applicant pool), inevitably some of those students would be in the bottom of the class. Therefore, about 25% of each class is chosen for its nonacademic qualities, on the theory that they will find their way to the bottom quarter and not mind being there, while still contributing with their other talents, and helping make the entire school more balanced. One of the most glaring examples of the Happy Bottom Quarter in action was a candidate admitted to Harvard whose only claim to fame (and one he stressed heavily in his application) was that he was in the *Guinness Book of World's Records* as the holder of the record for the longest continuous roller coaster ride (one which lasted several days).

All high school students should be aware of the distinction between Early Action and Early Decision. Early Action is a program sponsored only by Harvard, Yale, Princeton, and Brown. You can apply to one of the four in the fall; you are informed of the decision in the fall, and you have until May 1 to decide whether to accept. It is basically an early notification system for extremely promising candidates; an acceptance places you under no obligation. Except for Brown, it is probably not easier to be accepted Early Action than at the regular time. Early Decision is completely different. A large number of schools participate; you apply to only one in the fall; you are informed of its decision in the fall; and, if accepted, you *must* attend (other colleges will not review your application). Early Decision to college is American's version of Russian roulette: you can apply to only one school, and if they take you, you have to go; you will never know where else you might have been accepted. The bonus is that it does appear that it is somewhat easier to get into a college through Early Decision: the school feels good about you, since it knows you are very interested. In addition, Early Decision is used by smaller schools to snag candidates who might otherwise go to Harvard, Yale, and Princeton: Williams, Bowdoin, and Amherst, for example, fill ⅓ of their classes each year through Early Decision. But remember, you should be very committed to the school before you sign on, lest you miss opportunities elsewhere.

Finally, high school students should know that college admissions officers can be expected to scrutinize their high school transcripts quite thoroughly. High school curriculums throughout the nation are highly regularized, so colleges know exactly which courses are guts (known as "gases") and which are serious college preparatory material (known as "solids"). Admissions officers look favorably on all AP courses. They are wary of "Math/Science Bailout" in the latter years of high school, where an otherwise top student abruptly stops taking challenging math and science courses. When applying to colleges, it is definitely better to have a B+ average with the most challenging courses than all A's in speech, shop, drafting, typing, photography, drama, and soft math and science courses.

Law School

Law schools have the most formalized and rigid application system. Each school has a formula, developed by ETS, which is designed to predict first year grades. The formula weighs GPA and the LSAT, and produces an index number. The index number plays a very large role in candidate admission.

It is critical that applicants write well on the two pieces of writing that they submit. One is the personal statement. The other is the ETS writing sample. The ETS writing sample is not yet used heavily by law schools, but that time may soon be upon us. In format, the writing sample is very similar to a law school exam. According to the University of Wisconsin Law School, "Writing is so important to law study that we will give weight to [the LSAT writing sample], especially if it shows exceptional writing skill or weakness." There has been a rumor that a leading law school has considered taking all LSAT writing samples it receives and sending them over to the graduate English department for grading. Nothing of the sort has happened thus far, but such a development would not be entirely unexpected.

Most entering students either want to be business lawyers in a Wall Street environment, or legal crusaders for the poor and the downtrodden. As the latter is now out of fashion in the 1980's, expressing such unselfish goals is probably an asset in the application process, although only a very small one.

Business School

What is the ideal business school candidate? Business schools are looking for people who will go on to become successful managers. On the whole, there-fore, business schools take people who have already demonstrated some success in business. The schools do not believe that their job is to take people who have raw potential and turn them into managers. Instead, they see their job as that of taking people who have already had some business success, giving them some special analytical tools, and launching them back into the business world at a higher level. With that in mind, there are several ways to exhibit your business skills to an admissions committee:

Demonstrate that you have held a job with considerable responsibility. The more real business meat in the job, the better your chances: someone who supervised ten people is better off than someone who supervised two; someone who managed a budget of $500,000 is better off than someone who managed a budget of $50,000; someone who was an assistant to a corporate president is better off than someone who was an assistant to a vice-president, assuming companies of roughly the same size. How can the ad-missions committee assess how much importance your job has? In part, your recommendations may indicate the responsibility you have held. But in most cases the great bulk of information will come from you. If you can present your work in an interesting and articulate fashion, the admissions committee will believe that you had a job with importance and responsibility. It should be noted that it is becoming increasingly difficult to enter a top MBA program without prior business experience. For the class admitted in the fall of 1983, the percentages are given of the members of the class who came directly from college: Harvard (3%), Stanford (7%), Wharton (3%), and Columbia (20%). Even a few years ago, business schools were quite liberal in offering deferred admission to many college seniors: you were admitted directly from college, contingent on your finding two years of gainful employment. These programs went out of control, however, as some classes were half-filled two years in advance with deferred admits; now the reaction has set in, and some major schools do not offer them at all, or offer them only to minority applicants. If you are a candidate directly from college, you must explain how summer, part-time, or extracurricular work is, in your case an acceptable substitute for actual work experience.

Demonstrate that you have faced a variety of business challenges. In addition to showing that you have had depth of responsibilities, the admissions committee also wants to see that you have some breadth in your business experience. Business schools tend to frown a bit on applicants who are too rigidly focused toward a single career. You may have held a job since college at a Big-8 accounting firm, and plan to major in accounting at business school; that's fine. But if your application discusses nothing but accounting and shows no awareness of any business concerns outside of accounting, then you will have a problem. Admissions committees want to see that you have been exposed to a wide range of business situations. (If you plan to be a pure specialist, you have little need for the generalized training which business school provides.) Applicants who have worked for consulting firms, for example, are extraordinarily successful in gaining admission to business schools in large part because they have a wide variety of experiences to draw on in crafting their applications: they have usually worked with large companies and small companies, worked with manufacturers and service firms, and so on. Other applicants will want to show as much insight into a wide variety of business situations as possible.

Demonstrate specific things which you learned from your job.

Demonstrate that you have an understanding of the various disciplines taught in business schools: accounting, management science, organization behavior, finance, and marketing.

Demonstrate that you need an MBA to progress in your chosen career.

Demonstrate an understanding of the specific strengths of the business school to which you are applying.

Only the candidate who is able to meld all or most of these aspects together will gain admission to the best business schools, unless he has an extraordinary background not shared by the vast majority of applicants.

Graduate Schools of Arts and Sciences

Applications to the graduate departments in the arts and sciences is the most relaxed on the current scene. The most important factors in the process are the applicant's grades and his motivation to become a scholar. Almost always, the application is made to a particular department of a university. The chairman of the department and perhaps some faculty members may interview the candidate. The GRE may or may not be required, depending on the department and the school.

An important factor is research already conducted by the applicant. As an applicant, you are in an especially strong position if you have already been published. Recommendations from scholars in the candidate's field at the candidate's undergraduate university can be very helpful, especially if the scholars are well known.

Medical and Dental Schools

Medical and dental school admissions are the most frenzied on the American scene today. In a recent year, 42,155 pre-medical students applied for 15,774 seats.

Grades in pre-medical courses and the undergraduate GPA generally are the most important factors. The MCAT is of some, but not primary, importance. Work experience and extracurricular activities rarely play any role except perhaps to distinguish between two equal candidates. (Through some mysterious process it appears that children of doctors consistently have better chances of gaining admission to medical school.)

The interview is always the last step in the medical school admission process. The old high pressure interview now appears to be a thing of the past. The main purpose of the interview is to determine whether the candidate has the mental balance and stamina needed to become a medical student and doctor. A secondary purpose seems to be to gauge the candidate's seriousness about medicine.

Candidates who are willing to state that they will work as physicians in rural areas where shortages of doctors exist may have a slight advantage in the admissions process. All admissions to state medical schools are, of course, heavily restricted to state residents.

CHAPTER 6
Understanding the Admissions Officer: The Human Factor

A great deal of the admissions process rests in the discretion of the Dean of Admissions and his various assistants. Thus, it is important for the candidate to understand the general character of such individuals, and the effect that character may have on your application.

Money: Its Use and Misuse

As the first point of reference, admissions officers are individuals who have consciously forsaken the private sector and its greater financial rewards for a job they see, correctly, as having tremendous societal importance; thus, money is not a primary motivation in their lives. Therefore, if you are applying to college or graduate schools and are from a wealthy family, it is very important that you not flaunt this in the face of the admissions committee. For one thing, the committee will probably be made aware of it anyway; if you have not said anything yourself, you will get bonus points for being unassuming. It is correct to think that a university will be interested in your potential as a donor. However, the application is absolutely the wrong place to discuss or even hint about such a topic. There is usually a line somewhere in the routine portion of an application which asks for your parents' names and, perhaps, occupations. This should be more than enough to alert the admissions committee as to who you are; anything more detailed in your application should be avoided.

A corollary to this is that you should avoid overemphasis in your application on discussions of activities which relate to wealth, privilege, or exclusivity.

Many applications to colleges and graduate schools ask you to talk in depth about your most important extracurricular activity or about your three most important accomplishments. It is generally a mistake to talk in such a section about your involvement with your college fraternity or sorority, or your efforts on behalf of an organization like the Junior League. Granted, such activities are not in and of themselves handicaps; it is unlikely that an admissions officer will discriminate against you because you were a member. There is no reason why you shouldn't mention them as activities in a routine list, if you played some sort of a leadership role. The problem arises if you choose to highlight the activity as one of your most important achievements. Most admissions officers will consider it a questionable use of your time if, in fact, it was a major activity. They will ask whether it would not have been better for you to have spent more time on your studies. In their mind, for the most part, great involvement in such activities will reflect negatively on your values.

▫ **Case History #3**: **Sally Macintosh grew up and went to high school in a large city in the Midwest, where her family was very prominent. In that city the custom was for young ladies in society to make their debuts while in high school. The process of becoming a debutante was not purely social, however, but instead involved a huge amount of volunteer social work in the city. Sally not only fulfilled her quota of social work, she also became a leader in organizing the work of others. Sally was near the top of her class at an excellent high school in the city, and she assumed she would have no trouble being accepted to an excellent college. She applied to several Ivy League schools and several of the Seven Sisters. In her applications, she heavily empha-sized the good work she had done for the local debutante organization. The result, she was rejected at all of the major universities, and she ended up being forced to go to a much less rigorous small college, where she, of course, did very well.**

▫ **Case History #4**: **Frank Bingham was a pre-med at Harvard. He did not have spectacular grades at Harvard, perhaps a B average, but he very much wanted to be a doctor. Frank's greatest asset was that he was from Harvard, which is proud of its record of getting over 90% of its pre-meds into a medical school somewhere in the country. Frank's record was just a little below average for pre-meds at Harvard, but he planned to play it safe and applied to 15 medical schools at varying levels. Frank had been the vice-president of a final club, a social club at Harvard somewhat similar to a fraternity, and Frank had done a great deal of work in organizing social events and keeping the oper-**

ation running. So when he filled out his application he strongly emphasized his work at the club, along with some scientific research he had been involved in. The result: Frank got only one interview, and was rejected everywhere. He subsequently gave up his desire to be a doctor, and went off to look for a job in business.

The second important personality trait you should recognize in admissions officers is that they are essentially bureaucrats. Someone who becomes a professional admissions officer (sometimes affectionately called a "lifer") is interested in and loves being part of academia. Every admissions officer has chosen to become a bureaucrat, albeit one in a fairly pleasant environment. This must always be kept in mind when dealing with admissions officers: Form and punctuality are very important:

> "You are strongly urged to get an early start in the application process.... In many ways this is your first experience in preparing a case. As in most legal cases, it is important to be persuasive, clear, succinct *and timely.*"—Harvard Law School

> "Applicants are reminded that both men and women play active roles in all phases of life at the University of Minnesota Law School. Therefore, it is inappropriate to address the members of the Admissions Committee as 'Gentlemen.'"—University of Minnesota Law School

Throughout the application process, you should strive to do things by the book, as required by the admissions office, no matter how alien this may be to your personal ethic. This is not to say that admissions officers never make exceptions to their rules; they do, but only on their own terms.

The third psychological fact you should understand is that admissions officers are under enormous latent pressure. As the primary gatekeepers of society, they have an enormous responsibility to do a good job. On an individual level, they are well aware that they have the power to change lives (oddly enough, one psychological factor missing from the makeup of virtually every admissions officer is a strong desire for power). Yet they are never elected, and are not accountable in a direct way to the applicants whose lives they change. Usually admissions officers are appointed by a major dean of the university, and they basically serve at that dean's pleasure. That dean, potentially at least, can have an enormous influence on the policies of the admissions office and on its day-to-day operations. Thus, admissions officers are subject to potential pressure from three sides: society as a whole (expressed through public opinion, the news media, campus opinion, and faculty opinion); disgruntled unsuccessful applicants; and the university administration. It is no wonder that the Dean of Admissions generally keeps a very low profile on campus, and that the names of members of an admissions committee are very rarely publicized.

To add to this potential pressure, admissions officers are frequently subjected to real pressure: the pleas of applicants, their families, and alumni, that certain people be admitted. Many colleges are facing declining enrollments, and must now admit over half of those who apply. In those instances, many who apply pressure are simply let in. At graduate schools and Ivy League colleges, however, ten applicants for each spot is quite normal, and outside pressure comes down with special vigor. It is my belief that the great majority of admissions officers dislike outside pressure intensely, want to keep their independence as much as possible, and therefore fend off any pressure unless it is so great that they have no choice, or it is so mild that it doesn't seem like pressure at all. Clearly, if you can have the President or the football coach of the college of your choice call the Dean of Admissions and order you to be admitted, you will not have a problem. But if you are in such a position, then you barely need to fill out an application, and you certainly don't need to read this book. For everyone else, it is clear that the appearance of pressure will be a negative factor about you in the mind of the admissions officer, and therefore should be avoided.

The typical applicant should make the application speak for itself, and do nothing further. If you feel you are a borderline case on the record alone, and you know people who are in a position to and are willing to help you (obviously two completely different things), there are some rules to be followed: (1) All contact with the admissions committee should be indirect, unless the caller is a personal friend of the admissions officer involved. Nothing will hurt you more than an alumnus who is a stranger calling the Dean of Admissions and browbeating him about you. The proper thing for the alumnus to do is to call another dean or faculty member whom the alumnus knows, and make your case, which can then filter down; (2) Never have your callers demand that you be admitted. The alumnus should call, for example, the Dean of Students and say he is "interested" in seeing you enroll, would like to "check" on your admission status, and "is there any information I can provide to help the process along." The Dean of Students can then call the Dean of Admissions and say he is interested in your case; (3) Never threaten. If you threaten, the Dean of Admissions would love nothing better than to call your bluff. If you have been heavy-handed enough to threaten, the entire administration will rally against you and support the Dean of Admissions. In order to call your bluff, the Dean of Admissions will, of course, have to reject you first. So not only do you not get in, you and your family will be very embarrassed when you don't follow through on your threat; and (4) Someone helping you should be positive. He should continually stress your personal strengths, articulate that you would be a great asset to the school, and emphasize that his only interst is that you get "a fair hearing" before the admissions committee. At the end of your campaign, admitting you should appear the only fair thing to do in light of your outstanding potential and your ability to impress intelligent people, rather than the expedient thing for the admissions committee to do to get you off its back.

Finally, you should realize that the great majority of admissions officers are liberals, in the American sense of that word. I do not mean that they are all of the liberal wing of the Democratic party, or even that they are all Democrats (although academia did give Adlai Stevenson and George McGovern huge majorities for a reason). What I mean is that they are believers in the liberal ethic of equality and fairness. Everyone should have an equal chance in life; discrimination and racism should be eradicated; minorities and the underprivileged should be brought into the mainstream of American life; intelligence and character should be prized by members of society, not money for money's sake; individuals have a responsibility to society as a whole, not just to their own careers. Admissions officers are very rarely cynics; they enjoy helping people, especially young people, learn and get ahead, and are very conscious of the long-term social consequences of their work. Doubtless there are a few reactionaries among the admissions officers of the United States, but the prevalence of the liberal ethic is enormous.

One general result is the willingness with which affirmative action was adopted by universities in this country. Although numerical quotas are no longer allowed since the *Bakke* case, every significant college and graduate school makes special efforts to recruit minority students and special allowances to help them be admitted.

A more specific result of the prevalence of the liberal ethic is that you, as the shrewd applicant, should highlight aspects of your background which play to the social conscience of the average admissions officer. There are two basic approaches, which also can be used together. First of all, emphasize your personal triumph over adversity. Admissions officers are, I think, always willing to help the qualified applicant who needs a boost in life. Admissions officers are more than willing to play the role of the righter of societal wrongs, the balancer of the scales of life. If you come from poverty or are handicapped, you will have had to overcome disadvantage in order to gain an education, in order to be qualified even to apply for further study. That clearly reflects favorably on your character, and admissions officers will be happy to reward you for your past efforts. Remember that every college and graduate school admissions officer sees hundreds of files per week from middle class students who have dull backgrounds and are looking to go to school to make a career for themselves. Even the most enthusiastic admissions officer can only get a limited amount of satisfaction out of helping children of the middle class get a step closer to their ultimate goal of a $200,000 annual income. If you come along with a credible story of overcoming disadvantage, and can show that you can do the work the school requires, it makes the admissions officer's day (if not week or month) to help you get an education and a share in society's rewards.

Secondly, even if you do not come from a background of disadvantage, you can show the admissions committee that you have the proper system of values by demonstrating your social conscience and compassion for others. Usually, this is established through volunteer work and extracurricular activities which aim at helping others. You should realize that it is not good enough simply to list such activities on your application. What you need to do is highlight the activities so that they become one of the focal points, if not the centerpiece, of your application. You should not only describe the activity, but also describe your leadership role, and then use the opportunity to launch into a discussion of why it is important for someone like you, from a relatively privileged background, to spend a significant amount of time helping others less fortunate. It is my strong belief that even a relatively small amount of social work, if presented properly, far outweighs any extracurricular successes you might have in things like student government, school newspapers, athletics, fraternities, clubs, and the like. Being editor-in-chief of your school newspaper may mean you are smart, or ambitious, or a hard worker, but it does not make you a good human being to whom the admissions officer should give a boost.

Along the same lines, some extracurricular activities are better at demonstrating your compassion than others. Basically, the less middle class and mainstream the activity, the better. Working for the United Way, the Big Brother Program, the Jimmy Fund, or teaching Sunday school may be very worthy activities, but they are not going to create a great deal of excitement in the mind of the average admissions officer. They are very sanitized, safe activities which you can participate in with your friends and which are probably fairly easy and fun to be involved in.

What the admissions officer really wants to see is something unusual, a situation in which you have seen some real suffering first-hand and have put up with some hardship and inconvenience yourself. Let's compare two activities: raising $10,000 for the Jimmy Fund versus volunteering ten hours a week to clean rooms and prepare food at a men's shelter. Which activity has greater social value is entirely debatable and probably unanswerable; that the latter will have a bigger impact on an admissions officer, I think, is clear. Raising money for the Jimmy Fund shows that you have a good sense of values, that you can organize others to raise money, and that you work well with your friends. The latter shows that you were down in the trenches of society, facing misery and disease and suffering; you now have a keen understanding of poverty, and you were there to help those who most needed help. The closer you can come to helping people in immediate distress, the more vivid an impression you will make. Manning a counselling center for students is fine; staffing a crisis hotline is more vivid. Tutoring inner city schoolchildren is very good; going to a maximum security prison and tutoring lifers is more vivid. And visiting the sick or elderly is very noble; but volunteering in a mental hospital or an emergency room is more vivid. This may be unfair, but attempting to demonstrate compassion for others on paper is not a matter of how many hours you put in or how much you really care, but rather of how striking an impression you are able to make on an admissions committee, which often translates into how much unpleasantness you had to deal with and how much dirt you got under your fingernails in the process.

The Great Trap: The Pile of Mush (or, How to Bore an Admissions Officer)

A final psychological factor which you should be aware of arises not so much from the internal makeup of individuals who happen to hold such jobs, but rather from the working conditions of the job. A thread which runs through the life of every admissions officer is the boredom factor.

The basic job of the admissions officer, leaving aside interviewing and public relations trips to recruit students, is to spend 3–10 hours a day reading applications. Since admissions officers obviously only work for one school at a time, the questions to which the applicants are responding are always the same. In fact, schools often ask the identical questions for five to ten years at a stretch. The fact that the questions are always the same is bad enough, but the sad thing is that there is a terrible monotony to the answers as well. The same answers get rehashed over and over and over: "What I seek from a college is a stimulating learning environment which will enable me to reach my full potential as a human being...." "I want to go to law school because I want to work in an intellectually challenging profession while still helping individual people solve their concrete problems." "Only business school can give me the analytical tools I need to be an effective manager in today's increasingly complex environment." The majority of applicants' answers are stamped out of the exact same mold. They are the Great Pile of Mush— they convey very little information and have no redeeming literary value. The applicants who write such mush feel, either consciously or subconsciously, that the play-it-safe and "tell-'em-what-they-want-to-hear" technique is the best approach, and that the way to gain admission is to be so uncontroversial and bland that there is no chance that any member of the admissions committee will be offended.

This approach is absolutely the wrong one for any type of competitive admission process. (If the admissions process is not competitive, with 70% of all who apply being accepted, and you clearly have the proper academic credentials to be accepted, then a play-it-safe approach is quite sensible. But that is a very different situation from competition.) A dull, long-winded, play-it-safe application has all of the strength of a soggy piece of toast; you will quickly lose the attention of the admissions committee, they will think you are a poor writer (even though you may only have chosen a boring subject), and they will question your originality and maturity when they are forced to grit their teeth and read trite platitudes one more time.

Frankly, it often amazes me that more admissions officers do not quit their jobs to go mountain climbing in the Andes, or take to the bottle. The boredom ingredient must be incredible. As a result, any sparkle of excitement which greets the admissions officer's eye from the application's page is a welcome relief. Any admissions officer with any experience has seen all of the standard, routine answers hundreds or thousands of times. If you serve them up one more time, the best you can hope for is that he or she will stifle the oncoming yawn. But if you present something interesting, something unusual, something new, then you have made the admissions officer's day. He or she will have made a discovery: an interesting person who has something original to say. And I think you will be rewarded for being original and interesting, for breaking the monotony of the admissions officer's day. For one thing, you will get more attention at the admissions committee meeting (remember, we are assuming that you are in the Average/Borderline category), everyone will be sure to read what you have to say, and you will be differentiated from the great mass of other applicants. Generally, you will get bonus points for being interesting, original, witty, and so forth. And if the committee decides to put your file in head-to-head competition with another file, you have a strong immediate advantage because your story is more likely to capture the committee's interest.

One of the fundamental messages of this book is that original and interesting applications have a significant advantage over the play-it-safe and the routine. Always remember that the basic reason this is true is psychological: The admissions officer sees the pile of mush every day, several times over, and dreads seeing it yet another time. Help yourself, and preserve the admissions officer's sanity, by presenting something more interesting.